Dag Hammarskjöld:

STRICTLY PERSONAL

Dag Hammarskjöld:

STRICTLY PERSONAL

**A portrait
by
Bo Beskow**

1969
Doubleday & Company, Inc.
Garden City, New York

Library of Congress Catalog Card Number 69–10804
Copyright © 1969 by Bo Beskow
All Rights Reserved
Printed in the United States of America
First Edition in the United States of America

To My Wife, Greta

Contents

In my new official capacity the private man should disappear and the international civil servant take his place.

DAG HAMMARSKJÖLD 1953

The private man disappeared so successfully from public view, that when his biographers wanted the "human touch," they were stuck for material. To complete the puzzle they made their own home-made pieces to fit their pictures, or they fished bits out of the mounting flotsam of rumours and lies, so often repeated that they take on a false air of historical fact.

The picture of Hammarskjöld growing out of this "objective" writing seems so much out of focus to his friends, that I had to write this book. It may answer some of the questions too often asked me. But it does not pretend to give "the only true profile." Around the time of his death a few well-documented books were written on the Secretary-General (Joseph P. Lash, Richard I. Miller), and others will follow when more documents are released.

My sketch is of the man I remember. His letters speak for themselves, and so do the photos. The rest are scenes lit up in the twilight of memory. If they sometimes have a touch of autobiography, this is unavoidable. To be able to write I have to follow the flow of reminiscences, including my own doings at the time. However insignificant they may seem, small touches sometimes can add a lot to a large and complicated picture.

All comments on political situations and persons are my sole responsibility.

B.B.

Numana, Italy, June 1967

First Movement

In November 1952 Dag Hammarskjöld asked me to paint his portrait. He sounded nice over the telephone, but before accepting the commission I had to see what he was like. We met and had dinner and talked, and I studied him.

He was very clear and straight. He gave me the impression of moving around a vertical center line, like an old Egyptian sculpture or an Oriental dancer. In our Western classical ballet the dancers extend their movements to all the corners of a geometrical room, but a Hindu dancer moves around an inner axis and always returns to this. Dag moved gracefully around his center, but never farther out than that he could return to his core.

At that time I do not think that Dag had many friends among artists and writers, in spite of his great interest in their work. Later he could make his own choice among the great of the art world, but in 1952 that was not so. When I brought him together with some people he knew by name and fame, he seemed pleased—and everybody liked him.

In March 1953 we were ready to start on the portrait. Dag was the perfect model—far too perfect. I encourage my victims to move and be at ease and forget that they are posing. But Dag never for a moment forgot. Of course he was not supposed to see what I was doing, but somehow he guessed what my preliminary sketching was leading up to, and arranged himself accordingly. He kept a disciplined pose, a disciplined, nonchalant pose that nothing could shatter. I am sure he did so to be helpful.

Trying to catch him off guard, I kept questions going to keep him talking. I usually don't pay much attention to the answers, concentrating on painting, but this time I could not help being interested. I listened with one ear, and with growing respect for his great knowledge and sound judgment of art, theatre, music, ballet, literature, and politics. Our mutual interest in international affairs led us to question the future of the United Nations. We discussed the possibility of finding a good Secretary-General after Trygve Lie. Several names were mentioned—none good enough. It struck me that Dag would make a very good Secretary-General, and I told him so.

Dag smiled and said: "Nobody is crazy enough to propose me—and I would be crazy to accept." A few days later my morning paper carried a headline running over the whole front page: DAG HAMMARSKJÖLD NEW SECRETARY-GENERAL OF THE UNITED NATIONS?

Dag was due for a sitting on the same day, at one o'clock. He came, punctual as usual, and we talked. The portrait did not advance that day. I opened a fresh bottle of sherry and we talked for two hours. Since the last sitting he had hints and warnings about his candidature, and he had time to think it over. There was no doubt in his mind about accepting, even if he was a bit apprehensive. At that time I don't think he felt it as a heavy "duty" to accept—he saw the appointment as a challenge and a chance to do some really useful work. He was pleased and excited. I asked:

"Could you sleep at all last night?"

"Yes, of course—why shouldn't I sleep?"

"Well, if this happened to me, I wouldn't have slept a wink—or else I would have had terrible night-mares—dreaming that I was called upon to stand up in my old school, having forgotten my lessons—or standing on a stage to play Hamlet and not knowing my lines."

Dag smiled: "I never had dreams like that. I have tried to do my job and I have always slept well."

Good if this was true—a useful asset for a Secretary-General of the UN—but I silently wondered how long it would last. The hours went fast, and then I drove him down to the Foreign Office to meet the world press. He waved gayly as he went in to tell the world that he had accepted—and I drove back feeling that the sky was a bit higher.

We had a few sittings after that and the portrait was more or less finished, as a portrait of the man he was when I met him, not as the man he turned out to be. I would say that he matured almost overnight, being suddenly able to use and develop the whole range of his unique qualities. Our fathers both died that year, and I could well understand Dag's feeling of being free to be himself. Starting on a new life means cutting old strings and school-ties and making new friends. Having met at this turning point had something to do with our continued friendship.

Cleaning

Dag left for the UN and his oath of office. The problems he had to tackle were not only in the political field. On meeting the staff he said: "My first job is to run this house." Not an easy house to run, with its four thousand offices of more or less importance. To get the house in working order he had to do some re-organization. I have a feeling that everybody had expected—and some had hoped for—a less forceful person. He did not exactly swing the hatchet, but he wielded the broom with a firm hand. He had some cleaning to do. The house was slightly infected, not only by McCarthy spies and FBI agents.

It is by now a well-known fact, even outside the UN, that Trygve Lie resented the appointment of Hammar-skjöld. Not to seem biased, I prefer to quote Joseph Lash, who in his book on Hammarskjöld tells that Lie took the selection with ill grace: ". . . emerging, in fact, as the bitterest behind-the-scene opponent of the decision. —He turned white when Lodge came in on March 31, on his way down to the Security Council meeting, to say it was all fixed for Hammarskjöld and that the meeting would be over in short order. His disappointment vented itself in uncharitable references to Hammarskjöld. . . ."

Trygve Lie stayed on at the UN, keeping one of the rooms in the Secretary-General's office and making things difficult for Hammarskjöld. He continued with his "uncharitable references" (as Joe Lash so discreetly and carefully refers to them). The silly rumours that Lie spread reached Dag, who finally had to call him into his office and ask him to curb his imagination.

Dag cleaned the house, and in so doing could not avoid stepping on a few toes and making enemies (who after his death willingly furnished the biographers with material). But he also made friends and found much devotion to the cause, and when he returned to Stockholm for a short visit in the late spring, he spoke about his positive experiences and his hopes for the future.

We kept in touch by letters and he hinted at difficulties: "Here everything has been more hectic than usual (or reasonable) but things continue to work out rather nicely. However, I dream of private writing down at Hagestad after the five years of fighting here. *Then*, if ever . . . Before that you must come here—long before. Your room is ready."

Hagestad was the small village in the south of Sweden, where I helped him to buy a cottage near mine, and near the wild beach of Sandhammaren.

[17]

Hagestad

Around the south-eastern tip of Sweden stretches a sandy beach, which is a terror to all sailors and a delight to lovers of unspoiled nature and good swimming. On stormy nights the inhabitants of this dangerous coast used to walk up and down in the dunes, swinging lanterns. Ships out at sea, that were trying to round the cape, took the lights to be another ship and felt safe to draw nearer to the shore. None of the crew lived to tell the story, but God blessed the beach and the picking was good.

Ships of all kinds and from all centuries are buried in the forever shifting sand, and the fishermen sometimes catch very strange fish indeed. The hungry sea is continually nibbling at the beach and the dunes, and you are reminded of the words of the Bible (Job): "Hitherto shalt thou come but not further: and here shall thy proud waves be stayed." The fishermen have to drag

their boats far up on the sand every night, and they are always busy mending their nets, which crawl like prehistoric monsters on the white beach.

Behind the beach is a strip of wood, where foot-paths wind between wind-tortured pines and oaks on heaving sand dunes, where deer graze in the glades and a colony of herons cast strange shadows. At night the beams from the lighthouse of Sandhammaren sweep over the treetops, and on misty days you can hear the foghorn's muffled roar. A wild, lovely, and secluded country.

In 1945 I had bought a small, whitewashed, deserted cottage with a piece of land, on top of a steep sand-ridge above the wood. From my Rytterskulle I could see the horizon round the compass. Looking north I saw the fertile farming country stretch like a gigantic patch work quilt, dotted with white farmhouses and churches. Turning the other way I could rest my eyes on the unbroken line of the sea, satin-blue on summer days, black on stormy winter days, and at night hung with lights from ships and fishing boats. My piece of land gave me a chance to work with gardening, something I have always found necessary for my equilibrium.

I have described this hide-out of mine at such length, because it later pleased Dag so much, and gave him a few days of rest. When I told him about it, and my ef-forts to preserve this unique piece of Swedish land-scape, he got very interested. He knew the country from one of his bicycle tours, and he asked me if I could get him a place there. I liked the idea of having him as a neighbour, and I thought he could be very useful in helping to save the coast from exploitation. As a matter of fact I had long had my eyes on a cottage near by,

where an old couple lived who wanted to sell. It was situated at the edge of the wood—an excellent place for this particular kind of game-keeper. I had been waiting for the right person, and I told Dag I would approach the Jönssons with an offer, if he was interested. He had no chance to see the house, but after my description he told me to go ahead.

I bought the place in the summer of 1953, and also a piece of grazing land that extended from his house down to the wood. Dag did not see his place until next summer, but he had frequent reports of all developments.

The house was a whitewashed mud-brick cottage with a thatched roof, two rooms and a small kitchen, a barn later done over for a future library, and a hen-coop that was changed into a very pleasant guestroom. The thatched roof gave me a lot of trouble through the years—it had to be repaired and done over repeatedly, and it was hard to get the right kind of long straw. This had to be grown specially and thrashed by hand, by old people that knew how.

To start with I had only a few necessary repairs made and cleaned the house and garden. A new telephone line was installed, and from my herb-garden I transferred a few "herbs for healing and cooking": Mint for the stomach, Sage for the nerves, and *Melissa officinalis*, in Swedish called "The heart's delight."

Dag followed my negotiations, and later my efforts to put the house in order, with the greatest interest. In May 1954 I had for the first time a letter in English from Dag. His letters so far had been in Swedish, written in his characteristic hand and always in blue ink. He continued to write in longhand whenever he had a chance. He then felt free to express himself very candidly at times, as in talking to a friend without witnesses. From time to time, however, he had to dictate his letters, and then mostly in English for practical reasons. In these letters I feel a certain restraint, and sometimes an elaborate or amusing twist of expression, for the benefit of his secretaries, Aase and Hannah. And "warmest greetings," etc. were added in his own writing, when signing.

May 22, 1954—"If you are to get a letter at all with the very tight time schedule I am running at present, you have to get it in English as that makes it easier for me to dictate.

"Thank you for your kind and most welcome letter a few days ago. I was very happy indeed to hear from you. Let me also thank you for all the trouble you have taken in arranging the Hagestad business. The positive result (I hope no complications will arise) gives me much pleasure and I am looking forward to a very stimulating neighbourship. You know how much I like the Sandhammaren country which seems to provide a perfect refuge, not only when I manage to escape from here, but perhaps even more so when I get back to Sweden after the end of this adventure. I am sure we will find it possible to defend the area against intrusion. If people tend to be indiscreet we just have to kick them out firmly but politely. Anyhow, the sensation will wear out quickly.

"My hope is for the present to be able to come up to Hagestad around 20 July. . . . I will come from Geneva and in my company will be a young American who is my personal aide, a man I am sure you will like very much."

Rytterskulle

*My good neighbours the Jönssons
grew and thrashed the long
straw for Dag's thatched roof.*

This was the first time I heard of Bill Ranallo, who was going to become a good and wonderful friend. More about Bill later.

On the 17th of July 1954 they arrived at Rytterskulle, in Dag's rattling old prewar Citroën (which always kept Bill happily busy with repairs). From Malmö they had been guided and guarded by high police officers, who reluctantly drove off and left their precious charge to Bill and me. Dag rushed up on the highest spot of my land and stood there filling his lungs with the pure air, and his eyes with the unbroken horizon.

I gave them a substantial meal, full of strange Swedish dishes that I knew Dag would like. He was delighted. "Try this, Bill!" Bill tried—very carefully and with great suspicion. Bill never touched liquor when on duty, but Dag and I tasted spicy drinks flavoured with herbs from my old-fashioned herb-garden and we drove down to Dag's cottage in high spirits. We all had a feeling of being on a holiday-outing, and that nice relaxed mood stayed with us through Dag's visits. Most of the time—because there is no denying that he could be both irritated and irritating at times—in that respect he was a very ordinary human being.

He quickly took possession of his house and noticed all details. He liked the black old cast iron stove, with biblical scenes, and the few pieces of old farmers' furniture that I had put in the living room. He even accepted the rather hard, simple camping beds, that I thought could serve until he chose his own, more comfortable ones. He never bothered.

The kitchen I had equipped with the necessary pots, pans, and dishes, and with basic food and drink. Dag and Bill made their own breakfast, but otherwise they had all their meals on Rytterskulle; this simplified life for them, and was a rule ever after. Later Dag also brought his visitors and friends to the Beskow Restaurant —if he thought them worthy.

He quickly settled down to enjoy the two days' repose he allowed himself that time. Bill and I tried to defend the fort against more ambitious than tactful people of the press. When Dag left he was escorted by police to Malmö, and from Copenhagen I had a postcard:

". . . With the help of the police we reached Malmö where the hostile enemies renewed their attacks—."

Two Letters

On the 4th of August 1954 Dag wrote a long letter, full
of warm thanks and greetings. He continued:

"Here everything is as usual—which means great satis-
faction in my work and much nostalgia for free nature
and free humans. I think of your musical practicing at
Rytterskulle!

"Faulkner has published a book that is a monster but
still the most important in American prose since *Moby
Dick*. Partly unreadable, partly bewitching. All through
terrifying. What a strange genius and what a medium
for human passion and suffering. —A not unimportant
result of this book ought to be a new awakening of
the great ambitions in our friend J. and others. Provided he still can muster such heat as is required to
melt real poetry out of stone." [The book was *A Fable*,
and J. did muster some of his old heat, enough to finally
get him a Nobel Prize.]

From a letter of November 24 of the same year:

". . . Your letter from the studio at night, fell like rain on thirsty ground. I too am hungry for letters, nota bene if they are alive like yours.

"Maybe the period of re-orientation that you are passing through is a fruitful period—however dreary it may seem at the moment—a time of refuelling at the same time as you gain freedom. You have the curse of the artist to be your own master, I that of the slave always forced to solve 'given tasks'! Tertium datur?

"The pages of 'This I believe,' that you happened to see are not polite statements but deeply engaged ones, partly in self-criticism. They were written some-time last autumn but the last part says what I would say today: the counterpoint to this enormously exposed and published life is Eckhart and Jan van Ruysbroeck. They really give me balance and—a more and more nec-essary—sense of humour. My salvation is to 'take the job damned seriously but never the incumbent'—but it has its difficulties. The roads to a basic conviction that in the deepest sense is religious can be most unexpected."

Before continuing to quote from this letter I have to give a brief explanation. Dag had that year been elected as "one of the eighteen" of the Swedish Academy, an honour that you have to be a Swede to fully appreciate! He was to occupy chair number XVII, where he suc-ceeded his father. Following the tradition of devoting the installation address to the member you succeed, Dag was met with the difficult task of commemorating his own father, a very conservative man. In one of my letters I had asked him how on earth he was going to solve that "given task"—and in the light of all speculations about

Dag's attitude to his father, the following quote may be of some interest:

"The Academy speech is not attacking any myths. But it is strictly honest—an attempt at an all-through subjective analysis of motives. The picture is true—from a clearly stated aspect, that *also* is mine. Of course I have other aspects, where I myself stand in the center in a perpetual conflict with a dominating father-image (in many ways deeply unlike me) whose pressure I hated and whose weaknesses I consequently saw very clearly. But that picture tells more about me than about him and is in this connection outside the lighted area."

He went on to say that he could not stay in Stockholm after the Academy meeting; he longed for a few days of sun and swimming in the Caribbean Sea:

"Why don't you come here! And follow me South. The American tropical waters are worth a lot. In any case New York is not bad and I think I can bring together some congenial friends if you come!"

The Swedish winter was harsh, the Caribbean Sea sounded fine, we met briefly in Stockholm; but I could not leave. I had just met Greta. Dag on the other hand was sounding out the possibilities of going to Peking, in secret meetings with the Chinese ambassador in Stockholm.

Bill and Chou En-lai.

Chou En-lai and Bill

In January 1955 Dag flew on his first important political mission—to Peking. All efforts to bring about a release of the American airmen, shot down over China two years earlier, had so far been unsuccessful. Dag decided to go to Peking and talk to Chou En-lai, officially on the strength of a resolution in the Security Council in December 1954.

"I go to Peking because I believe in personal talks—I can only say I will do my best."

The story of Dag Hammarskjöld's best is well known by now. He took great chances, knowing that a failure would mean a further lessening of confidence in the UN and the Secretary-General. But he also saw an opportunity to restore the weakened prestige of the organization. Not many expected him to succeed, and when his quiet diplomacy for obvious reasons could not show immediate result, his critics triumphed. However, faces were saved and the airmen were released in due time.

On February 12 Dag wrote:

"The China voyage was a fantastic experience. I feel in a sense more grown up than before. Colourful and exciting, infinitely distant and still terribly real. This goes both for the country (the landscape), the atmosphere of Peking (this magnificent camp for nomadic rulers who have come down from the desert over the narrow mountain-ridges—a camp with an infinitely repeated rhythm of burdened tent-roofs), and Chou En-lai himself (with a brain of steel,—strong self-discipline and a very warm smile).

"This goes also for the unreal voyage 'around the earth in 7 days.' Not forgetting the human and political problems where I suddenly was alone holding the knife. Such a situation relieves you of the last traces of an 'I' which later does its utmost to push forward again!

"My working team was first class. Bill was great and he saved the morale both in my professors and the others when the wind blew so sharp that only the most open, simple human sense of humour and warmth could prevent frostbites.

"I am very cramped for time but I have begun to read again in earnest. And I really am able to read, in a way that gives results—and this seems to show a tendency towards balance."

"Bill was great." Yes, Bill was great, and I would like to quote from a later letter, of November 1955, after Dag and Bill had spent a whole week with us in the summer. (Greta and I had married in March, and at that time Dag wrote:

"I am sure you are doing right—my warm, very

warm congratulations. I feel that you now sail into freer and brighter waters again.")

On November 12, 1955, Dag wrote:

"You ask where is the human warmth? Everywhere and nowhere. In my situation in life I suppose this is part of the price of the stakes, that you are able to give yourself wholly and without reservation only if you don't steal, even in the smallest degree, from someone else: really to 'die' in the evangelical sense, that is so frighteningly realistic as a description of the situation of man—can at certain times force you to this paradoxical egoism. ('Who is my mother and my brother, etc., etc.') Instead I have the light and easy warmth of contact with friends such as Greta and yourself, or, for example, the Belfrages—or Bill: a kind of comradeship under the same stars where you ask for nothing and receive so much. —When I see other possibilities (like yours), I can feel a short pain of having missed something, but the final reaction is: what must be, is right."

The Belfrages and Bill. Greta and Leif Belfrage were —like Eva and Per Lind—unfailing friends from the Swedish Foreign office, and generous hosts whenever Dag came to Stockholm. I am afraid they would resent my even trying to tell what their warm friendship meant to Dag, but I do think the time has come to say something about Bill.

William Ranallo was a police officer who had been Trygve Lie's personal aide-de-camp, and who continued to watch over Dag, and at the same time make life easier for him. Bill really was quite a wonderful man— even if he was very unlike Dag. Nobody could accuse Bill of being intellectual, but he had sound views and

[37]

very good intuition, besides having a warm heart in his big body. Dag trusted his judgment of people, and was very dependent on his practical way of solving all sorts of problems and situations, domestic or international. On most photos and news-reels showing the Secretary-General arriving at or leaving airports or shaking hands with Kings and Queens and Prime Ministers and other VIPs, you can in the background see a kind but watchful face, always anonymous. Being anonymous and unobserved, Bill could watch the great of this world from unsuspected angles; in moments when they did not play up to Hammarskjöld he could note their side comments and uncontrolled faces. Later Dag could ask him: "What do you think of X or Y?" Bill usually confirmed Dag's opinion of how far he could trust them.

Bill was a dark-haired, rather heavy man. He had Italian blood, but was very very American, in the way nice Americans can be. He loved life: food, women, hunting, swimming, children, animals. He carried a service gun all the time, but had little use for it. I know few people that get along so well with everybody as Bill did. Walking through the UN building with Bill was a parade of smiles and greetings. When not on duty he sauntered along in his slow way, with a joke or a friendly word for everybody. He hated quick walks, but strode manfully to keep up with Dag when on duty. He had great tact—however informal we all were when alone, he was the perfect official aide when the situation required it.

He drove Dag from 73rd Street to the UN every morning—he was on duty all day and sometimes all

*Bill keeps an eye on Khrushchev
while Nina blesses the handshake.*

night—and then drove him home again. He supervised the household, helped the cook to decide the menu and prepare dinner when Dag had guests, and up at Brewster and in the cottage in Sweden he ran everything. God knows how he had time for a private life—and his sweet wife Toddy—but somehow he managed.

He died with Dag in the crash.

The Hunting Lodge

On the 23rd of July 1955 Dag came to Hagestad again—this time to stay for ten days, as things turned out. He and Bill arrived rather late at night. It had turned pitch dark. I was busy in the kitchen when I heard the familiar rattling and explosions of the old Citroën. The headlights appeared over the hill, but not where I expected them. In the dark Bill had taken the wrong road, or rather a bumpy track that ended in a potato field. The noise in first gear was terrific and the lights danced around and hit everything but the ground as the Citroën bravely took all the hurdles. It bumped over the potato field and came to a long-deserved rest in a sandpit on the highest point of my grounds.

I rushed up the slope to rescue the victims of the crash and was met by roar of delighted laughter from both Dag and Bill—it was all part of the fun of being here again. Fortified by the waiting supper and my

healthy herb-spiced concoctions, we later somehow managed to put the Citroën together again and turn her around, so that she could roll downhill to the Hunting Lodge. We had started to call Dag's cottage the Hunting Lodge ("Jaktslottet" in Swedish) after the books of Jonas Love Almquist, the great Swedish nineteenth-century author, a favourite of us both and also related to Dag's mother. I sometimes wrote to Dag in the delicate style of "Herr Hugo," and having used the name of Jaktslottet for Dag's cottage, the name stuck, to everybody's bewilderment who was not in the game.

Greta had been away to visit her family, but came the next day and was immediately accepted and loved. Dag called her "Ondine," and Bill taught her to shoot. We made a happy family and the days passed quickly. As did the occasional thunderstorms. On sunny days we swam and played games on the beach. Luncheon was usually served in the shade of the old apple tree, and dinner was quite a ritual in the small candle-lit dining room. I like to remember Dag's sun-glowing face at the other end of the table, an old wooden table, worn smooth by many generations' elbows.

We took long brisk walks. Bill hated this part of his duty and was always on the lookout for something to stop Dag:

"Look, sir, what bird is that?" or "That is a strange flower, sir, have you taken a photo of it?"

It worked most of the time—Dag always carried a camera—and we could all have a chance to breathe for a moment. Otherwise Bill did not care for flowers. After a week of sharing household duties in the Hunting

Lodge, Bill one morning came up to us, alone and in a very black mood:

"Do you know what the crazy S-G did this morning? It was his turn to sweep the floor—and do you know what he did instead? He went out to pick flowers! *Picking flowers!*"

But on the whole, things went smoothly, and one day they decided to invite *us* for dinner for a change. This took a whole day for preparation, with long mysterious trips to nearby towns. And what a dinner! Dag had set the table with beautiful old silver and candles, and the room was full of flowers, arranged by a loving hand. (Not Bill's!) Bill put all his love in the food and almost all of himself. It was a shining and proud Bill that staggered in under the antipasto—enough to feed a regiment. He really was a good cook. We sang: "*E noi che figli siamo—beviam beviam beviamo*" until late in the quiet night.

I don't think Dag ever did any gardening himself, but he was very interested in my herb-garden, and listened amused to my learned lectures on how to make life easier for your friends and harder for your enemies, by putting into practice the old knowledge from the time of Dioscorides and the Borgias. I had by patience and stealth and wealth acquired about fifty of the most useful and interesting herbs that thrived in the sandy soil. Plants with a long long history and a long long list of virtues. For the delight of your bowels, your nervous system, your heart, and your brain, but most of all of your gustatory nerves. Dag loved my aquavit spiced with wormwood or *Artemesia abronatum* or—the best of all if you had the patience to wait five years—the

Bill gets a chance to breathe.

"Ondine" in her ceramic workshop.

deep red and exquisite brew of *Hypericum perforatum*, that "drives out the Devil and maketh women warm."

He also followed with understanding my perpetual war on the moles, who always were up before me in the morning and had a rumpus in the garden. I never knew what they would leave of my most tender and precious plants. At first, on catching one, I carried the velvety monster far out in the fields of my neighbours, and I used rather humane methods of warfare—but my wrath mounted until it was a question of their lives or mine. We buried them with honour under a white rosebush—quite a ceremony. Dag had a painting of mine, "The Burial of the Mole," in the Hunting Lodge—and he often referred to the moles symbolically.

[48]

On board the m/s Navada of Gislöv.

Birthday

People from the Swedish press were at times trying to be, what they thought, very American. Bill and I had difficulties in keeping them away. Later I walked with Dag up and down Manhattan without the slightest trouble, except an occasional glance of discreet recognition. But on Dag's very rare and short visits to Sweden, to get a few days' rest, he was pestered by photographers and journalists who would not take "No" for an answer and who almost climbed in through the windows to take candid shots.

This kind interest in his doings seemed to be culminating in the days before the 29th of July, when he was going to reach fifty years of age. Greta and I made plans to give him an undisturbed day. We did not tell Dag or even Bill about our scheme, but we had their blessing. I only asked Bill to bring Dag over to our place early in the morning. If I remember rightly eight o'clock seemed early enough to fool the early birds of prey.

In the nearby harbour of Kåseberga we had found a skipper on a fishing craft, who was willing to take us out to sea for the day, for a reasonable compensation. He was from another port, and had put in temporarily with his *Navada of Gislöv*. He knew neither us nor our guest, and had no reason to spread the news.

The day started fine with a beautiful morning, calm and sunny. Bill brought a sleepy and slightly suspicious Dag—he was never at his best in the morning—but his mood improved with the morning coffee and the huge traditional birthday-cake. When we drove him down to Kåseberga he began to look expectantly amused and when we had boarded *Navada* and were chuff-chuffing out to sea he was grinning happily.

We were supposed to fish cod and were soon very busy trying out all sorts of tackle and tricks. The skipper smiled innocently; I have a suspicion that he took us to places where no cod ever went, because we did not catch a blessed thing. We soon gave up, all except Bill, who felt his honour as a sportsman at stake. Greta had packed a picnic-luncheon that was laid out on the hatch. The sea was calm and blue, the sun was pleasantly warm, we toasted Dag in a tolerably nice claret, and all was well with the world for the moment.

When we had had enough of sea and sun and absent cods *Navada* began to draw near to shore again. The setting sun lit up a strange scene in the little harbour of Kåseberga, that we had left sleepily deserted. It now looked like a beehive—evidently the news had spread somehow. The hills around the small fishing village were crawling with people, mostly females of all ages and shapes, who rushed to the pier when *Navada* put in.

Bill is suspicious of the tackle.

A toast in claret.

They were cheering and singing in honour of Dag, and the cameras clicked as he plowed his way through the crowd, waving and smiling his polite official smile but dark in the face. "Let us get out of here quickly!"

We drove back to Rytterskulle and barricaded the doors and had supper by candlelight. The press stopped in the dark outside the windows and reported next day that we had given Dag a very frugal meal in our primitive cottage. The cottage was primitive all right, but the supper was not altogether frugal that night. One of the main dishes was a gift to Dag from friends in Moscow, a two-pound can of Russian caviar, eaten with big spoons, as caviar should be eaten. If you have the chance once in your life!

A huge pile of mail had arrived; we brought it down to the Hunting Lodge and watched Dag open letters. Some came forwarded and collected in large fat official envelopes from the Foreign Office; but most were what Dag called "crank-letters." In New York letters of that kind were mercifully stopped from reaching him, and this time they took him by surprise. He evidently had expected letters of quite another kind, but the people he hoped would send greetings seemed to have been too discreet. Instead he had an avalanche of loony messages: marriage-proposals and money requests and all sorts of crazy advice. I remember that one anxious lady warned him against eating cold food, because the Bible teaches you that you shall eat your bread "in the sweat of thy face."

Dag began opening his mail in an expectant mood, but his face was a study as he opened one letter after another and threw them on the floor in disgust: 'Crank-letter, crank-letter, crank-letter!" In the meantime Bill in his corner was reading a pile of accumulated love-letters from his Toddy.

I don't remember if the telegram from Chou En-lai came that evening or the day after, and I don't remember its exact wording, but its meaning was: "Happy birthday—I am releasing the American airmen." The official publication came later and was of course more formal. But this personal greeting with its good news was the right kind of birthday gift.

Suez

In the summer of 1955 Hammarskjöld had given three university addresses of great importance for the understanding of him and his office. Talking about "international service" at Johns Hopkins University, he said:

". . . There is no formula to teach us how to arrive at maturity and there is no grammar for the language of inner life. . . . Apparently easy successes with the public are possible for a juggler, but lasting results are achieved only by the patient builder. . . . Those who are called to be teachers or leaders may profit from intelligence but can only justify their position by integrity."

At the University of California he stated:

". . . It has rightly been said that the United Nations is what the member nations make it. But it may likewise be said that much depends on what the Secretariat makes it."

*Greeting the first U.N.E.F.
troops (Danish and
Norwegian). Abu Suweir
Airport, November 17, 1956.*

Hammarskjöld was no juggler, and he was patiently building up his office and laying the foundation for the Secretary-General's duty and power to act quickly in situations of crisis. The Middle East crisis was growing to alarming size, and he was not content to sit in his office and receive reports from the areas of trouble.

In the end of January 1956 he left for an extensive tour of the Middle East, Asia, and the Pacific, visiting Turkey, Israel, Egypt, Lebanon, Jordan, Iran, Syria, Iraq, India, Burma, Thailand, Indonesia, Australia, and New Zealand. On his return he gave a press conference (February 27), where he sadly commented on the limited power of the UN: "We cannot intervene with force now—maybe later."

He hoped that the Security Council would give him more freedom and power to act, but it evaded the issue, and when he was requested by a resolution on April 24 to return to the Middle East "and report back not later than one month," he commented rather drily:

"It is obvious that this request neither detracts from nor adds to the authority of the Secretary-General under the Charter."

He left again for Israel and Egypt on April 6, and these trips were only the beginning of an endless series of hurried, tiresome, and politically difficult travels through the following years, to areas of unrest and danger. He certainly had use for his quiet diplomacy, in private talks with touchy heads of state, whose faces had to be saved if any solution should be reached. For obvious reasons the result could not be announced on his return. He could tell his friends and collaborators in the Secretariat that the fever-crisis was passed and the temperature going down, the wildly speculating newspapers got an official version later, but very few knew what really had happened. Too few realized how often he foresaw a coming crisis and was there in time to lift the lid from a pot in danger of boiling over.

Like a chess-player he saw many moves ahead and acted accordingly. His quiet diplomacy included the responsibility to keep confidential talks to himself, and sometimes also to keep quiet about the results until the time was ripe. I was amazed over the cocksure editorials in some Swedish newspapers during the Suez crisis. The fantastic story of the Suez has later been told so well by others, and I have no reason to dwell on this. But it was a great day for an old World-Federalist, when the first truly international police-force in the history of man, the U.N.E.F., was magically set up in forty-eight hours!

On June 2, 1956, Dag wrote: "You know the reason for my silence too well for me to give any explanations. After my return from the more and more unbelievable expeditions to the Middle East I have had terribly much to do and decide and—honestly—I have had a tremendous need of sleep. I suppose that the true and exhaustive account that I would like to give Greta and you, has to wait until evenings at Rytterskulle, when they with some advantage may be given by Bill. After all 'reporting' I am not, as you surely understand, in any mood for storytelling. I can only say that this whole business is an unbelievable, partly shocking experience. It really has been good to hear from you both—from your sound world with stained glass and weaving, May-nights and Sandhammaren. Most of all thanks for what

you tell about yourself. Hagestad is a firm landmark. . . ."

He gave himself no rest—for long periods he had
almost no sleep at all. He hoped to have a few days in
Sweden, but on July 26 I had a wire: "Visit to Sweden
cancelled—reasons obvious—." But his letters continued to
come:

September 15—"From my existence there is as usual
so much to tell; that nothing gets told. There is an
infinite struggling and taking of risks, in accordance
with the motto that Erik Lindegren has given: 'Catch
Death!' In a sense without reward, 'dangerous' at least in
that sense that you so easily lose yourself in the wrong
way, but still so very much worth while and stabilizing.
You get however a strange impression of humanity and
history. On the whole 'true,' I suppose, but not complete
since human warmth is rated so low on the stockmarket
of these 'Men of Action.'

"I often think of your stained glass windows and
your preoccupation with the eternal problems of the
space of the canvas. I hope I will still have enough of
patience, humility and stillness left when one day I
shall be allowed to return to a life along the same lines.
Then, maybe, I should be able to say in the right way
something of what should be said.

"The world is slightly mad, and the more you are
compelled to witness this, the more you long for good,
wise friends in a quiet nook, where you don't listen to
the radio and are more interested in the migrating
birds (that probably by now, passing Rytterskulle, have
returned to the frogs in the Nile (not minding Nasser)."

*"I know this sounds ridiculous, but I
can't help feeling they're trying to tell us something."* ✗

✗ They do: That Bill and
I hope to come round
the 25 July for a few
days, but that everything
depends on the Swiss
manoeuvres (alas!).

Dag

SSS GENEVE 28/27W 25/7 2202 ETAT

BO BESKOW LOEDERUP SWEDEN

VISIT TO SWEDEN CANCELLED ~~STOP RETURE E E~~ STOP RETURN NEWYORK
THURSDAYNIGHT STOP REASONS OBVIOUS STOP AWFULLY SORRY BUT ONLY
POSSIBILITY STOP WARM GREETINGS TO BOTH

DAG

October 20—"—As usual I am behind with my letter-writing. Thanks for your long, stimulating letter. Strange how a small corner of Österlen more and more feels like home, with Greta and you as its good guardians and life-givers. 'Världen är så stor så stor, Lasse Lasse liten.'

"Suez was my third child. The parents arrived in a state of great bewilderment and some fury. God knows how this will end—but the brat cries less now and perhaps, with good assistance, I can teach it to walk. (Your characterization of Krishna Menon is absolutely right: he is the whimsical, self-important Aunt who runs around bothering everybody.)

"The other day I gave Dr. Fawsi the following description of the situation:

"Tragicomedy in three acts:
Act 1. The Secretary-General is chaperone (a passed stage by now).
Act 2. The S-G has shown some talent to appear on the stage as a (helas, so moral) procuress. (This scene is still to be written.)
Act 3. The S-G is allowed—with good luck—to try his talents as a midwife.

"The end all right—everything all right—but what are they going to say about the S-G?

"Palestine is a complete mess. In the shade of Suez and the American election the Israelis have seen the chance to arrange things in their favour—as they believe. But I am afraid they will have to pay one day. With the sympathy I have for them *on one level:* it hurts me to see them, on another level, behave in a way that I have

A letter from Dag.

20 okt. -56.

Käre Bo.

Som vanligt är in på efter-
böljorna med min tacksägelse.
Tack för Ditt långa o trevliga
brev. Lustigt hur så litet här
av Öckerön alltmer känns i en
kommer med Greta och Dig som
den goda väntan och längtan-
re. Världen är så ... så ... bara
bara liten — "!

Sorg blir inte tråkig bara.
Frisältvar kan bli i sin tillf-
stånd av ... väldi... och
...yn iskla. God ... kan det
gör — man ... skri... min...
... och in kommer, med god

to condemn officially. Not because of what this means in the way of trouble for me, but because of the split in Israel that it shows and which may once more cause them unhappiness.

"Saint-John Perse is a great poet. But he has to be reread many times and with absolute surrender to his intellectually strongly disciplined furia. His French is difficult."

This was the first time that Dag mentioned Saint-John Perse, pen-name for the French diplomat and poet Alexis Léger, who some years later was the Nobel Prize winner in literature.

Dag had already at this point found the only possible way to rest a brain overheated by unsolvable problems: to tackle something very difficult in another and quite different field. His problems were too great to forget by "relaxing," but he could rest some brain-cells by using others. "His French is difficult." A nice challenge to Dag. He translated Saint-John Perse's *Chronique* into Swedish, and while doing this struck a personal friendship with the poet. Their admiration was mutual. In Dag's copy of *Œuvre Poétique* Saint-John Perse wrote:

"*À Dag Hammarskjöld*
—Magicien."

Back to Suez. Dag used to say: "I know we cannot solve any of all these problems definitely, we can only try to prevent a catastrophe for the moment." The Suez crisis passed its dangerous peak and was settled in some state of control of the symptoms, for the moment, but the sickness itself still remained, ready to break out again sooner or later.

On June 4, 1957, Dag wrote:

"I am slightly less harassed now but instead some tiredness is creeping out of the corners where it has been hiding through the winter. At any moment something may break again. We live in a rather insane world and it certainly does not get the wiser from the reckless (or rather shameless) propaganda it has to suffer from well-known quarters. If people only would remember the true words of Fröding 'that nobody is bad and nobody is good,' they would be able to immunize themselves against this propaganda picture of a world with villains and saint-like martyrs, observed by cold-blooded persons who for unknown reasons want to please the villains. This simplification is however so tiresome in the long run, that possibly we may return to realism. One can hardly maintain the viewpoint that everyone who finds *some* good to say about Nasser, or *anything* to disagree about with Ben-Gurion is anti-semite—and consequently crypto-nazi. Well, let us hope for a spiritual self-healing. And let us keep ourselves sane!"

I am sorry to say that the "well-known quarters" included some of our leading newspapers in Sweden. It was quite *en vogue* in so-called intellectual circles in Stockholm during the Suez crisis to criticize Hammar-skjöld and the UN and poke fun at "the sweet little boys in blue caps that play soldiers in Gaza." The stupidities overheard at dinner tables and read in editorials, could not be explained by ignorance only. There was a strange element of malice and spite towards Hammarskjöld personally. Maybe the notorious Swedish envy had something to do with this.

The rather bitter and sad letter ends on another note:

"But why talk about this—when the sun is shining over the hills of Kåseberga and the problems of form call for a solution, we will forget the distortions of a world that we ourselves have created."

That year Dag had a very specific problem of form, which, indeed, called for a solution: the Meditation Room in the UN building. The Meditation Room was created before his time, but Dag felt that it needed a complete redecoration to serve its purpose. His great interest in art led up to this.

The Arts

Dag's interest in art and music had in his younger, pre-UN days a leaning towards the romantic. He occasionally bought a small painting—mostly a fine-toned romantic landscape by some good if not great Swedish painter. By the time he was appointed Secretary-General, his taste had began to develop into a deep understanding of quality. During his time in New York he was more and more looking for the kind of simplicity that is a result of a long process of eliminination, and built on a foundation of great experiences and knowledge. He avoided artists who take shortcuts, those who think that loud noises and blown-up sizes show greatness.

In all performances of art he grew sensitive to the hidden reserves, that make you feel that an opera singer is using only part of her resources and can hold her high C forever if she wants to. He knew the training and discipline, the endless and hard practicing that makes

Speaking in front of a painting by Léger.

a good ballet dancer or violinist, and he understood that painters and sculptors are no exceptions from the rules of all creative art.

To his home on 73rd Street he brought some of his romantic landscapes from Sweden. He added art of another kind, for example the beautifully simple drawing by Matisse over his writing desk. The first nonfigurative things were, if I am right, a Barbara Hepworth and one of my sketches for the mural in the Meditation Room, both in his study.

In January 1954 he selected some paintings from the Museum of Modern Art, to be hung in his rooms on the 38th floor of the UN building. Some of them were changed later on, but this first list may be of interest:

Peter Blume: "The Boat"
Lyonel Feininger: "Viaduct"
Fritz Glarner: "Relational Painting"
Juan Gris: "Guitar and Pipe"
Henri Matisse: "Gourds"
Pablo Picasso: "Still Life with a Cake"
George Rouault: "Landscape with Figures"

I think this first choice proves my point. The works of Blume, Feininger, and Rouault are definitely on the romantic side, which of course does not exclude quality. He later added beautiful pieces of Eastern art, primitive art, and non-figurative art to his office rooms. In the dining room at the UN he had very few things: a "Single Form" by Barbara Hepworth and a small graphic study in geometrical space by me. (Members of the "Congo-Club" have told me that he used to gaze at those two while he was thinking.)

In his address on the 25th anniversary of the Museum

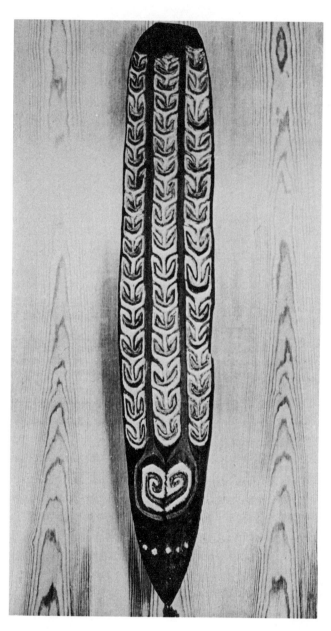

North Guinean Warrior shield.

Sculpture by Barbara Hepworth

of Modern Art, on the 19th of October 1954, he said:

". . . there are two qualities which are shared in common by modern art and the scientific sphere: One is the courage of an unprejudiced search for the basic elements of experience. The other one is perseverance in the fight for mastery of those elements. . . . One of the great composers of our age has said that the artist must start out, again and again, from two colours or three notes or the right angle."

This last quote is from the Danish composer Carl Nielsen's charming little book, *Living Music*, of which I had written to Dag. I like to quote Carl Nielsen more fully: "Nothing is so embarrassing in all art as false originality. —Oh ye artists! Learn that the smallest shall be the greatest, that two colours, three notes, two right angles and a circle are enough for him who has reached the true happiness in working as a humble servant in the world of art."

Dag often compared the problems in art and science with those he encountered in his own field of work—a philosophic and moral comparison. About that time Robert Oppenheimer said at Columbia University:

"What does the world of arts and sciences look like? There are two ways of looking at it: One is the view of the traveler, going by horse or foot, from village to town, staying in each to talk with those that live there and to gather something of the quality of its life. This is the intimate view, partial, somewhat accidental, limited by the limited life and strength and curiosity of the traveler, but intimate and human, in a human compass. The other is the vast view, showing the earth with its fields and towns and valleys as they appear to a camera

With Ben-Gurion.

With Israeli children.

carried in a high-altitude rocket. In one sense this prospect will be more complete: one will see all branches of knowledge, one will see all the arts, one will see them as part of the vastness and complication of the whole of human life on earth. But one will miss a great deal; the beauty and warmth of human life will largely be gone from that prospect."

Like Oppenheimer, Dag had a unique combination of detachment and engagement, being warmly engaged and at the same time keeping a certain distance, necessary for keeping a sense of proportions—and his integrity. This "distance" was misunderstood by people who wanted to "get near" to him. As soon as he had a chance, he was a traveler going by foot from village to village—but he never lost "the view from a high-altitude rocket." The village side is not generally known; the public has seen him *ad nauseam* in mass media on official occasions, where he appears politely smiling with the VIPs. But on all his whirl-wind travels around the world he managed to have moments in better company: with children in Israel, with farmers and artisans in India, playing, tasting domestic wine and bread, trying his hand at the tools of handycraft. "The man knowing man, the neighbour, the schoolboy learning a poem, the women dancing. . . ." (Oppenheimer.)

On those occasions he seems for a moment to have thrown off his burden of office—being himself.

In the film-library of the UN I have seen hundreds of thousands of feet of film with Hammarskjöld, many of them from his visits to Asia and Africa. The Swedes would hardly recognize him—somehow they never accepted that the student from Uppsala turned into a man of international thinking, feeling, and living.

He was a true world-citizen—with an interfaith philosophy. This added to his interest in the Meditation Room of the UN.

The Meditation Room

When Dag in June 1957 told me he would try to come to Sweden for a few days, he added: "I have a plan that I am very eager to discuss with you."

He arrived with Bill on June 29, drove as usual straight to us, got rid of the police escort, plunked down in a deck-chair, accepted a drink, and said: "You will have to come to New York in August." I answered that I could not leave my garden at that critical point of the summer, it needed my constant care to survive attacks from insects and weeds. But when he told me about the Meditation Room, my objections were overruled.

The idea of a place for interfaith meditation and prayer somewhere in the UN came up after the plans and construction of the buildings were so far advanced, that this had to be crammed in as an afterthought. Through the efforts of the "Friends of the Meditation Room" a corner was finally found, and the room was pushed, like an almost triangular, thin piece of cake, into the west corner of the public lobby in the General Assembly Building.

The Friends had tried to do their best with this rather dismal and curiously shaped room; the result was such that it was a challenge to Dag. He had started by cleaning it out completely, shortening the room by erecting a screening wall at the entrance, and lowering the ceiling by hanging a second ceiling with hidden lights. From Sweden he had, as a gift from a mining company, a block of iron ore, beautifully proportioned and with a lovely surface, that caught and reflected the thin beam of light from overhead. This stone seems to be floating in space in the middle of the room. People working or passing in the basement workshops or underground garages wonder what a heavy concrete pillar is doing there. It supports seven tons of iron ore in the Meditation Room! Like the hidden underwater strength that carries the sunlit peak of an iceberg. Finding this out gave me a most unusual and comfortable feeling of solid quality in a city of wear-and-throw-away mentality.

Behind the iron-ore block, in the narrow end of the room, a slightly projected piece of wall descends from the "hanging" ceiling. When you first enter the room it seems pitch dark—the only thing you can see is the upper surface of the stone. If you manage to find a chair without tripping over somebody or something, and sit there for a while, your eyes, ruined by city-glare, begin to get accustomed to the soothing half-light. Your eyes travel beyond the stone, and formerly they met a blank wall, where they and the fantasy stopped.

The Meditation Room.

Dag felt that something had to be done to that wall. To this end he and the architect, Wallace Harrison, and their advisers from the Museum of Modern Art, approached some of the great French masters (Villon and Braque, if I remember rightly). They, however, refused to come over themselves in order to execute something on the wall. As the UN had earlier experiences of small sketches being sent over to be enlarged and executed by others, Dag insisted on an artist who was willing to come in person and be "married to the room." He proposed me. At that time I was not very much known in the United States—and there must have been some discussions. Our friendship was not the main reason for Dag to mention me; he had had opportunity to follow my work, and he knew my intentions. He would never propose anybody unless he thought him the right person. That was the way he worked: he gave a free hand and great responsibility to the right person to do a good job —and you had to do a damned good job!

As he described the room and its problems and function, I could not help being interested. This was just in my present line of work—I had had a long period of not exhibiting—being more or less breaking away from the past in more ways than one. For ten years I had been wholly engaged in problems of space, the geometrical room, inter-changing forms and planes, dynamic symmetry, etc. In other words, I was learning to know my grammar better.

"If you come you will of course stay with me," Dag said, and when I accepted on the condition that I could bring Greta, he explained apologetically: "Well, there *are* two guest rooms, but I am afraid you two will have to share the same bathroom."

This frightful prospect did not prevent us from coming to New York on the 12th of August, and we stayed with Dag in his flat on East 73rd Street until the middle of November, with an interval for completing some work of mine back home in Sweden.

The morning after our arrival I drove with Dag down to the UN for my first rendezvous with the Meditation Room. Not only was I married to it—I was buried in it. It was a dark vault without air and light, and certainly not a room of "quiet and stillness." The thin walls let through the enervating tap-tap of women's heels on the stone floor, of guides' and visitors' blah-blah, and the unguarded door let anybody through to see what was going on. I had a wonderful man from the basement workshops, Bill Kolberg, to help me with practical things, and he fought bravely to keep people out and to get me some lamps, working desks, and a chair. That chair took a whole day to produce, since it needed a written, official request passing from bottom to top to be approved and signed. After having taken a chair from another room, and kicked some Very Important Persons out, we got into trouble, Bill Kolberg and I, with some of the middle-bosses of this amazing organization. I finally had to tell Dag about the situation, and a charming topman with undersecretary's rank was called in from his vacation. He told me he had given up smoking and gave me a pipe. I also got two security guards and the right to ask for things I needed.

Home in Sweden I had built a small scale model of

the room, from the architects' drawing, and had done some preliminary sketching. These sketches were useful as an approach to the problem, but now I covered the wall with paper and started to construct my composition in full scale. I found my task to be that of trying to open this closed room, using the measurements and planes of the iron-ore block for a geometrically controlled "movement in space," giving the eye and mind freedom to travel, and giving some simple forms to fasten on for meditation, serving the same purpose as the crystal ball of fortune-tellers.

Dag was very tactful, and did not bother me much while I was working. For some reason I did not feel disturbed when he did let his curiosity take the upper hand; and when I finally presented the finished sketch he said: "This is what the room needed."

The architect, Wallace Harrison, was asked to see the result. One of the nicest men that it has been my luck to meet, Wally came, sat his tired body at full length on a chair, and looked. Silence. I walked nervously around the room, offered cigarettes and sherry, and waited. I could not stand the suspense any more: "Wally, for heaven's sake say something!" Wally gave me a surprised look. I was disturbing him. He had already started to meditate!

So far so good. But this was only a sketch on paper. I intended to execute it in fresco, the unsurpassed technique for murals from the days of the old masters and still done the way it was used by Piero della Francesca and Uccello. To my surprise this technique seemed to be a lost art in New York, and I could not find an old-fashioned plasterer to prepare the wall and be my assistant. My hunt for one, in this city of steel and concrete, led me to strange experiences, and I almost gave up. I knew that the Mexican painters had done good fresco work in New York, in the twenties and thirties, but they must have brought their own helpers and material.

The maintenance department of the UN did not understand what I was talking about. I have studied and practiced this technique more than most of my colleagues, almost down to the point of stirring the colours with a twig of an olive tree, as Cennino Cennini recommends! I knew how the wall should be prepared, and asked to have it done, the way I wanted it. No, it was not that simple. The whole machinery began to grind, endless discussions on all levels took place, "experts" were called in, and finally I was triumphantly presented with an imposing paper on "How to paint in fresco." Luckily the chapter on "How to prepare the wall" corresponded more or less with my humble requests from the start. Dag was amused and said: "You see what I am up against sometimes." I finally found an old plasterer who remembered something from his youth, we all agreed on how to prepare the wall, and while this was done we had an interval in Sweden. When I returned for the final execution, we took up living with Dag on 73rd Street again.

The entrance hall.

At Home on 73rd Street

Dag of course was a perfect host. There is an old Italian saying: a guest is like a fish—after three days he stinks! The prolonged and repeated stays of a married couple in his bachelor flat must have taxed his patience hard. But Greta being what she is, it worked out nicely.

I always had a feeling that Dag's real home at that time was the 38th floor of the UN. But he had turned the two-story flat on 73rd Street into a charming place —maybe more aesthetic than comfortable. I am reluctant to describe it in detail, maybe because I knew the details too well, from the listing and packing of his things after his death.

However, some of the photos I took will help to convey the atmosphere. We liked his study best, with the immaculate writing desk, his selection of books, his music-corner with the hi-fi, and his favourite reading-chair.

His household was well run, by the cook, Nelly, of Swedish origin but international in her art of cooking, and the butler, Ivar, from Finland. Both great characters, with an unfailing loyalty to their master and his needs and moods. (Dag had deep respect for Nelly and her sovereignty over the kitchen-department!) Those two had considerable help and advice from Bill, and the alternating personal aide Donald Thomas, a quiet and soft-spoken man, of great charm and efficiency. (After Bill's death Don took over at the UN, and is now the mystery man behind U Thant in photos and news-reels.)

We quickly entered into the rhythm of the house. In the mornings we found Dag in the spacious living room, reading the New York *Times,* and consequently in a bad mood, especially if there were reports from the UN doings. (No shadow on this excellent paper—it could not help the usually bad news.) He tossed the mastodon paper at me and said: "Read this!" Sometimes it was impossible to know what I was supposed to read and react to, but with some training I managed to find the offending piece and make a suitable comment.

Dag was not one of those gay early birds who sing in their bath and greet you with disgusting cheerfulness, making you feel doubly awful. The mornings were not his best time of the day—and I sympathized deeply. Explorers have told me that when you draw near to the shores of Borneo at sunrise, you are startled by a ghastly wailing from the jungle; you can hear the monkeys protest against being born again to a new day of hardship and terror.

We had a quick, frugal, and probably healthy breakfast

at the vast table in the dining room—gobbling our sour-milk to keep pace with Dag. If I reached for an extra bun with my coffee, Dag's eyes went to his wrist-watch. Every morning Bill and Don came in the big Cadillac to drive us down to head-quarters, Dag and I. We arrived in great style, smartly saluted by the guards. Later I heard that there were wild speculations about the mysterious bearded VIP who arrived every morning with the Secretary-General, carrying a most impressive attaché-case. Fortunately nobody looked into my case—they would have had the surprise of their lives.

As far as the guards were concerned the mystery was soon solved, thanks to Bill. A friend of Bill (and Hammarskjöld) was a friend of the whole house—or most of the house. I was accepted as a member of the UN family and had free passage, including the 38th floor, that otherwise is a well-guarded fort. I could go there and rest when the Meditation Room was a headache. Probably the only person who went there to *rest*.

The Secretary-General's office suite at one end of the long corridor is a little world of its own. It was at that time inhabited by Andrew Cordier as Chef du Cabinet, Cordier's secretary Doreen, and Dag's two secretaries: Aase the fair Norwegian and Hannah the dark Dutch girl, good-looking and efficient ladies. There were Bill or Don, if Dag was in his office, the coloured butler, and Loretta in the telephone-exchange. She knew every voice in the house and could locate anybody in no time. On my first visit Aase was presiding at the imposing desk in the center of the secretaries' room, Hannah

*The Study: The music corner
and Dag's favourite reading-chair.*

The writing desk.

Pladz later took over, and also followed Dag on his long African tour.

In the opposite end of the corridor Ralph Bunche had, and still has, his office—and in between you find several of the top-men of the UN. A friendly and stimulating place, besides being a place of unbelievably hard work. My free passage included the General Assembly and the Security Council, were I often dropped in to listen to the debates, and not for a moment could I forget the strain and worry that night and day followed Dag, however composed his behaviour.

We did our best, Greta and I, to help him forget for a moment now and then. In this we succeeded best on Wednesdays, when Nelly and Ivar had the afternoon off, and we made surprise dinners for Dag. And what surprises! There are wonderful food-shops on Madison Avenue, where you can get anything from French cheese and Russian caviar to bees fried in their own honey, and the best meat in the world. Shopping was a pleasure—and so was cooking in the well-equipped kitchen. Usually Dag was late for dinner and arrived tired and dejected, causing Nelly and Ivar some worry over a spoiled dinner. But on Wednesdays he came home early, in an expectant and good mood. This really is no boasting on my part—I think he was amused and touched by our efforts.

What did we give him to eat? Well, I do remember my pleasure in serving him heads of champignons, stuffed with well-spiced and creamed chicken-liver, with a touch of old brandy, and au gratin. After these Wednesday-dinners Dag rushed out into the kitchen-department to wash dishes and clean up, in spite of my protests. When

I cook there is certainly some cleaning to do afterwards, and I had no intention of doing it. I longed for a comfortable chair and a good cigar after the day's hard labour—and I really thought that Nelly and Ivar could take care of the debris in the morning. No, we had to go to work.

And here I would like to comment on the way writers make the most absurd statements about Hammarskjöld. In one of the later efforts I read to my surprise that he was not good at washing dishes! Really! Facing the risk of being taken seriously, I must protest. For the sake of history I feel it my duty to correct a gross misstatement on this evidently important point: he was extremely good at washing dishes—he was in fact the most perfect dishwasher I ever saw in my long life. He was a super dishwasher, even *singing* while he performed this dreary task, which always spoils the fun of cooking. Nelly could not find a speck next morning.

When Dag did not have to return to the UN or was otherwise not engaged, we usually sat in his study after dinner, often listening to music or hearing Dag read something he liked; classic or contemporary authors and poets. Sometimes letters from his many friends in the international literary world, or a translation he was struggling with, or a draft for a university or academy address.

Sometimes there were guests, and Dag was a charming host. He had the rare ability of reading between the lines, of listening to what was *not* said in a conversation, and he hated false pretensions, even when brilliantly displayed. Then the signs were unmistakable; his shoulders rigid, one foot tapping impatiently and the

The view from Dag's writing desk.
In the sofa Per Lind.

Baby Webster burning and smoking at a furious pace. When such guests had gracefully been escorted to the door, Dag said: "Well—that was that!" and went into his study. Home in Sweden he would have opened windows to let in some fresh air, but in an air-conditioned and polluted New York he had to resort to other means. He went to his collection of records and our ears were cleansed by listening to a fugue by Bach, or Ezra Pound's magnificent reading of his own stanzas or a folk-song, sung by Kathleen Ferrier, a voice as clear as the flutes in Laos.

These dinners could also be great fun and take unexpected turns. Once we all went downtown to Basin Street to listen to exclusive jazz. It was a place of worship, a young, very serious, public filling it to the breaking point. We were squeezed in somehow, happily anonymous in the darkness. But of course Dag was spotted, and when Stan Getz climbed the podium, he made a speech for Dag and in his honour played a syncopated version of a well-known Swedish folk-song: "*Ack, Värmeland du sköna.*" Applause, and a bowing and smiling Dag, who whispered: "Let us get out of here before the press comes." Next day the gossip-columns carried the story of Dag Hammarskjöld's devotion to jazz, proved by his visit to Basin Street in company with high officials from the UN. As far as I know, this was Dag's one and only jazz-session, and the suggestion was not his. It was Wally Harrison's, who likes things to happen.

Basin Street had given Greta taste for more, and we went to some of the good old jazz-bars when we were on our own, exploring New York. I found a sadly changed city from what I remembered from the thirties, when I had last known it. Gone was the elevated on 3rd Avenue, gone was my old friend and colleague The Tattoo King, gone were most of the small oyster-bars. But Washington Square still had its Henry James atmosphere, the art galleries had multiplied, and Alfred Barr, Jr., was still a landmark of culture at the Museum of Modern Art. I sometimes left the Meditation Room for an art-round with Greta, and Dag was always interested to hear what we had found. He took us to his favourite restaurants, where he was well attended to, but never bothered or stared at, and we had a few haunts of our own, of less fame but not less good.

He seldom accepted a private dinner invitation, and then only with friends. At the house of Bill and Toddy he was gay and relaxed, on other dinner occasions more self-conscious and a charming center of attention. We met some very nice people. At the Harrisons we dined with Kitty and Robert Oppenheimer. We all sat in respectful silence, listening for great words between two great men. They seemed delighted to meet, but slightly hampered by the audience. At one point of the evening I happened to say to the Oppenheimers, that so far I had been only to city homes, and mostly those of millionaires, and that I longed to sit in a farmer's kitchen. Robert Oppenheimer smiled and said: "Come to us in Princeton—we have a farmer's kitchen." Later we went —Greta and I.

One evening-at-home we tried on all Dag's magnificent academic gowns and caps and Oriental mantles and burnouses. I especially liked a gift from King Saud, a lovely soft brown burnous with a flowing white headdress; it brought out the sheik in me. Next day an American author and his wife came for dinner, old friends of mine that I had introduced to Dag. I dressed up in the King Saud magnificence, the lady was enchanted to meet royalty, and not until I gave her a big *embraço* did she recognize me among the folds. She has never forgiven me.

Dag took us to the theatres and movies. One night we took a chance on the nearest playhouse, and sat through two long Wild West stories, with Red Indians and the virtuous bar-whore and all. I suggested that we leave after the first film, but Dag would not hear of it. The theatres he chose with great care. I especially remember a performance of *The Iceman Cometh*, that was one of the best I have ever seen. Dag's interest in the theatre had always been great. A former editor of the leading Swedish literary magazine has told me that they once asked him to be their theatre critic.

His interest in good writing is well known. After dinner we often walked down to the nearest Doubleday book-store and browsed among the latest publications. Dag always carried something home to read—something new and interesting, to add to his library if it was good.

He was a "constant reader." He knew his classics, but was also always on the look-out for what was happening in contemporary writing. When I painted him in 1953 we discussed the answer to an old question: Which ten books would you take with you, if you had to live on a desert island for the rest of your life?

I don't remember the exact list that we more or less agreed upon. It included obvious things, like *Divina*

Dag's office on the 38th floor.

Commedia, the Bible, the collected works of Shakespeare, etc.—but I also remember *Spoon River Anthology*, Hesse's *Das Glasperlenspiel* and, on Dag's suggestion, *Le Rivage des Syrtes* by Julien Gracq. The list would surely have looked different towards the end of his life, maybe fewer well-known classics and more of the less-read philosophers? My guess is that Martin Buber would have been included.

Dag was a constant and hungry reader. After his death, as we were listing and packing his things, I found on his bedside table the following four books (the manuscript for *Markings* already taken care of):

An Introduction to Haiku, by Harold Henderson
Poems of Gerard Manley Hopkins
Poems, by George Seferis
The Way and Its Power, by Arthur Waley

Of course this did not mean that they were his favourites; he had happened to be reading them before leaving for the Congo and Ndola. To my knowledge he never read a detective-story to lull him to sleep, nor, of course, science-fiction. I think he regarded moon-rockets and space-ships as a waste of time and money.

We saw the first Sputnik pass over New York, and Dag remarked: "This will mean a complete change of strategy of the cold war. But it will take some time before people realize this." Pause. "And many years before T. does it." T. was at that time chief editor of Sweden's leading daily newspaper; for some reason he thought himself a great authority on politics, war strategy, the wrong-doings of the UN and especially of Dag. About

From the Secretary-General's dining room.

In conference with Ralph Bunche.

With Cordier and Boland.

this time Dag had been re-elected, and T.'s editorial comment was a masterpiece of perfidious spite.

The re-election was a vote of confidence for Hammarskjöld and his office and a great personal success. We were in Sweden at that time, and when we returned we found a slightly more relaxed and hopeful Dag. He even had time to write an address on Carl von Linné for the Swedish Academy. Most of the draft was written in the General Assembly, during a marathon speech by a certain Indian delegate, who put everybody else to sleep and then fainted, keeping up his faint until all the photographers and he were satisfied. The whole show obviously for the home market; as so many unnecessary speeches in the UN.

Dag now and then gave small luncheons for selected guests, in the Secretary-General's dining room on the 38th floor, and at other times I joined him in the excellent restaurant of the UN. I learned to know his nearest collaborators rather well—and many others. I think my friends will understand if here I only mention Andrew Cordier, the solid rock foundation of the Secretary-General's office, and Ralph Bunche, who for many is synonymous with the UN. As I write this I feel a nostalgia for the UN. In spite of all the changes I have seen on my later visits, the friendly atmosphere prevails. In spite of all the unavoidable tension, it is a good place to work in. Dag made it so—and U Thant continues, wise and dedicated. (I happened to be in the house when U Thant took over, quietly but firmly quenching the aspirations of those who had hoped to profit by a more lax reign. I heard him take the oath of office, and later had talks with him in the "private-talk-

U Thant in Stockholm
(*browsing among my books*).

corner" of old. I may have expected to feel some kind of sad resentment over the change, but I was happy to have a nice feeling that the UN was very lucky indeed.)

Weekends were a special problem. At times Dag could manage to get away only for a brisk walk, if he could get away at all. One cold windy Sunday we hunted at a furious pace all over a deserted Manhattan for an open flower-shop and a white cyclamen. Dag was absolutely set on a white cyclamen, nothing else would do. But this was not a day for white cyclamens in New York. We returned cold and wet and frustrated, and Dag set his shoulders rigid and said: "Never mind. It isn't important at all. *Really*—I have other things to do. I have to go to the UN." When we came down for dinner Dag was back, very occupied and concentrated on reading something in his favourite corner. Beside him in the study stood a beautiful white cyclamen.

All was well, and the guests could arrive: Mr. and Mrs. Erland Waldenström. Dorothy is a very beautiful and charming woman, and I could understand Dag's day-long hunt for a perfect white flower. He was aesthetically a perfectionist, and I see nothing wrong in this.

On weekends when Dag was all tied up, we went off on our own. With the Harrisons to their place on Long Island, to shoot clay pigeons with Paul Hammond and his sweet wife, and see Wally's first exciting models and sketches for the new Opera House in Lincoln Center. We went to the Steinbecks in Sag Harbor for barbecues and seagoing and fun in general. And to the Oppenheimers in Princeton "to eat in a farmer's kitchen."

But whenever Dag felt he could leave for a day, we drove up to Brewster, on the chance of his not being called back immediately on arrival to tackle a new crisis, as happened some of the times.

Brewster

Some two hours' drive north of New York he rented a pleasant white colonial-style house, with a lovely view, a garden, and a small lake. Four bedrooms, two bathrooms, living room, and a neat kitchen. There was also a guest-wing, never used by Dag, chiefly because the wife of an earlier tenant admired Pollock, which in itself is a nice thing to do. But with her it had resulted in the spilling of thick colour in spidery designs all over the *floors*. Which hurt both your eyes and your feet.

Bill or Don drove us up, the car loaded with provisions, packed by Nelly under their stern supervision. Dag always sat in front beside the driver, usually in a nice excursion mood. Also very talkative. On those occasions I had a strong feeling that he overrated my hearing-powers and my intellectual capacity. Those that have sat behind Dag on the way to Brewster will recognize the situation. With a Baby Webster in one

Bill and Dag on the road to Brewster.

corner of his mouth and a mumbling Oxford accent in the other, he would throw names and book titles and quotations in all languages at you without turning his head. Catch as catch can. Usually the radio was on, and a Cadillac of some years' vintage, going at full speed on a highway, is not soundless. You had to lean forward and strain your ears and rack your brain and make a guess, and find something noncommittal to grunt, that might fit in if your luck was good. I used to catch Bill's eyes in the back mirror and get an unmistakable wink, of deep sympathy and understanding.

On our arrival Dag and Co. with the routine of long practice set up the household in no time. Those of us not already comfortably dressed, changed into slacks and sandals, drinks were served and food prepared. Depending on the time of day and season, we walked down to the lake to have a swim and wash off the city dust. The lake was straight out of my childhood's Red Indian stories; quiet, mysterious—a dark unruffled pool with overhanging trees—Injuns and turtles watching us with unblinking, ancient eyes.

On the rickety landing stage lay a battered Canadian canoe. We launched it and paddled out to a raft in the middle of the lake. This raft had its own nice story. When the house at Brewster was put in order for Dag, by a crew of men from the UN workshops, he was so popular with them that they wanted to give him a surprise treat. This took the form of building a fine raft, which was presented to a deeply touched Dag. To show his appreciation he invited all the workmen and their wives to a big garden party. "And can you imagine," as one of them told me, "the Secretary-General himself served us all food and drinks, seeing to it that everybody was happy! He is a wonderful man Mr. Hammarskjöld."

We had our cooling swim, and if time permitted, a drowsy rest on the raft. Now and then Dag went fishing, but when he one day really caught a poor little fish (to everybody's surprise), he had to call on Bill to take it off the hook.

Our dinners at Brewster had a picnic atmosphere, with all sorts of improvised happenings and improvements on Nelly's food. Afterwards we sat on the terrace

in the dark, warm nights, with fireflies dancing and crickets chirping. We rested horizontally in Dag's "irrigation chairs" that fed the brain with blood—with some help from an excellent brandy. For some reason we were able to pick up what we had missed on the drive up, and the talk flowed easily.

If we had a next day, we played badminton and practiced archery. One weekend I bought a cheap movie camera in a drugstore, and some fancy animals, thought up an unwritten manuscript, and produced my first and

Don Thomas and Dag.

so far only movie-picture. Dag of course was the noble hero, a green fuzzy drug-store monster called "Charlie the Terrible" was the villain, Greta played the Damsel-in-Distress, and Bill was a more energetic than successful dragon slayer. For myself I had chosen the modest part of a cowardly Duke. It turned out very nicely—Dag acted his part with great grace and dignity. "With my bow and arrow—."

Leaving Brewster was always a sad affair. Packing, cleaning, burning the garbage—and then back to town in a suffocating Sunday-night traffic jam. Once, on the way to New York again, Dag said: "When I keep going day and night without stopping, I somehow manage. But after a weekend like this it seems impossible to face what I have to face at the UN." He was at that time under a ferocious attack from "well-known quarters."

Maybe his interest in the Meditation Room helped him a little to keep his equanimity. Whenever he could spare a moment he came down to follow the slowly growing fresco work. When it was completed at the end of October, he seemed to be very pleased with the result.

The great day came for the official re-opening of the Meditation Room, on November 8, 1957. Dag gave a very nice luncheon on the 38th floor, with a selected gathering of heads of museums and foundations. Everybody enjoyed the food and gave nice speeches, everybody except the artist, who felt terrible. I am never more down than on these occasions; having finished an absorbing job and having to show it and listen to praise, that however kind seems to have no connection with your work.

[113]

Don Thomas, author and Dag Hammarskjöld.

Dag and Greta.

Dag and Greta.

The next day we left for Sweden, I to pick up my sadly neglected work there. The friends of the Meditation Room had their room back—it took some time before they accepted the changes—but then extremely nice letters and press-comments and stories began to reach me and warm my heart. I especially liked the story that one of my friends in the Secretariat told me. He had escorted two Jesuit fathers there; after two hours of contemplation they came out and asked my friend: 'Why hasn't the artist painted the star of Bethlehem? We saw the sun and the moon and the Saviour on his cross—but . . ." They saw what they wanted to see in this purely nonfigurative mural—and that is what I hoped for. This happened after Dag's death. He would have liked this confirmation of his own words:

"There is an ancient saying that the sense of a vessel is not its shell but the void. So it is with this room. It is for those who come here to fill the void with what they find in their center of stillness."

My studio at Christmas time.

Christmas 1957

Dag came to Stockholm to give his address on Carl von Linné at the Swedish Academy, on December 20. The day after, I gave him an improvised Christmas party in my studio. He was told to bring anybody he wanted—and we were quite a crowd of friends.

My studio in Stockholm is big and old, with great tradition and a tree-shaded garden. The night of the Christmas party I stuck flares in the heavy snow-drifts—the black tree-trunks stood out like sculptures, with branches stretching forth welcoming and blessing arms. I stood on my balcony and saw Dag arrive with some friends, including Bill and George Ivan Smith. He stopped and threw his hand out: "Look at this!"

In the studio a long table was set, ready to receive an army. On a separate table all the mysteries of traditional Swedish Christmas-food were displayed, including a pig's head, fancifully decorated. (Christmas in Sweden

*George Ivan Smith—"with a face
like a sunset over a sheepfarm".*

is rather a hedonistic cult around the pig.) A row of bottles gleamed in the candlelight and a richly adorned Christmas-tree gave forth a nice fragrance of pine needles and candle wax. Soon everybody was red cheeked and shining, beautifully matching the polished red apple that was stuck into the mouth of the pig.

For the sake of Bill and George Ivan everybody spoke English. An elder brother of Dag looked surprised at junior, leaned over the table, and whispered to me: "Doesn't he speak Swedish any more?"

Bill was as usual deeply suspicious of the pagan Swedish specialties, but George Ivan loved it all, as he loves most things in life, including brown goat-cheese, raw herring, and smoked pig's head with sugar decorations. This kind and brilliant and very civilized Australian "with a face like a sunset over a sheepfarm" (O'Brian), was later to be one of the many UN civilians in the Congo, who fought madness with patience and bravery. Together with Brian Urquhart he was arrested, beaten, and nearly killed by the "paras." To quote an eyewitness: "—George Ivan Smith with his face swollen and holding his cracked ribs together with both hands, directing, advising, restraining, imperturbably at the centre of everything until the moment he fell."

But that was later—much later. My dear George, how far we were that night from Katanga and Ndola—no paras or Fougas roaming the darkness outside.

A few days later Dag was in Gaza, to spend the Christmas with the UN forces. Dag in Gaza, familiar with his Bible, must have felt the span of history, repeating its pattern:

And the border of the Canaanites was from Sidon; as thou cometh to Gerar, unto Gaza, as thou goest unto Sodom and Gomorrah—.

Like Philip, he had followed the command from the Angel of the Lord and gone "unto Gaza, which is desert."

And who shall declare his generation? For his life is taken from this earth.

The desert, terrifying most people, must have fascinated Dag. Even if Sodoms and Gomorrahs were lurking all around, he loved unbroken horizons. That is why he bought Backåkra.

The Admiralty

When I looked westward from my Rytterskulle, I saw
no houses, only gently rolling hills along the coast-
ridge. About a mile away a grove of trees marked a
habitation. My walks often took me there, to the almost abandoned and ruined old farm, with its wide view
over sea and plain. Its ninety acres of grazing land was
like a magic carpet of green velvet, strewn with millions
of small flowers of the heath. The house itself was an
old fortress which time has passed by, it was built in a
square around a closed court.

Backåkra had passed through many hands and fates.
In the original deeds it was called Fårbacka (Sheep-
Hill), but the pastoral sight of grazing sheep was no
more. The owner at this time was a man living in
another village, who kept pigs in what was left of
stables and barns, and in the remains of the corps-de-
logi lived a strange out-cast family, dark and wild and
shy.

Looking over the sea from Backåkra.

Among Dag's most appreciated and visited neighbours were "the Stones of King Ale".

When Dag joined me in my solitude, I took him up there. We could stand forever and get our fill of silence and vastness, and the sweet smell of the heath, mingled with pine and sea. Somehow the sky seemed bigger there than ever. The both wild and peaceful beauty of the place attracted Dag immediately, and he knew of my dream to be able to buy it in the future.

Backåkra was suddenly put up for sale, and in danger of being sold to housing speculators, who raised the price. I had not the money to fight them. I tried to get the Nature Preserving Authorities interested, and succeeded in this, but still we could not raise the money. I wrote to Dag about my efforts and my worry, and when he came to Sweden for a few days in June 1957 he told me he was willing to buy it. By shock tactics we managed to get the price down, and in two days the deal was a fact—in principle.

On July 6 Dag wrote to his Swedish lawyer: "On my recent visit to Sweden at Hagestad, I engaged myself in a new development, on which I need your legal assistance, in order to conclude negotiations and establish the necessary documents etc.

"Prior to my visit Bo had been in touch with all the Authorities in Stockholm and locally, and it was obvious that they would not only approve of, but might even welcome, the purchase of the estate by somebody who is willing to put it under a 'servitut,' providing that the land must not be built upon or cultivated but left an open heath. —Bo had himself had in mind to buy the estate. However, the farmer had then asked for the somewhat exorbitant price of 120,000 kronor, which stopped further efforts. In the course of my visit I made an offer to the owner. The price I mentioned was 70,000 kronor. It was accepted right away—."

On July 25 I signed the contract for Dag, and "the necessary documents etc." began to pile up into a dossier on Backåkra, that continued to swell through the coming years. Now looking through the thick files of bills and letters and contracts and resolutions and legal papers of all kinds, I am surprised that I managed to do anything else beside worry over Backåkra, and supervise its restoration. My reward was Dag's enthusiastic replies on my reports: "I try to console myself with the thought that you regard Backåkra as your own creation."

For some reason Dag did not like the name; Backåkra means Hilly Acres. The old name of Sheep-Hill did not please him either. Having read *Le Rivage des Syrtes*, I began to call Dag's new house "the Admiralty." A place where Dag, like Aldo, could escape the intrigues of The Signoria, and in the quiet of the old fort by the sea shape his philosophy and feel the unrealness of the never declared and never ended war between Orsenna and Farghestan. Dag liked the allusion, and from then on it was the Admiralty—in our correspondence.

At that time you could not buy a farm in Sweden without being a farmer, or getting special permission. I had told Dag that he had to suggest putting the estate under certain nature preservation rules as an excuse for buying it, otherwise he could not get permission. Which was partly true. On March 17, 1958, we finally had the official resolution on this.

One clause excepts "an area of one acre in the northeastern corner of the estate, which said area eventually can be disposed for a chapel—."

[129]

The Admiralty ready to receive Dag.

As this clause later got to be known, and has caused some misunderstandings, I must explain what was behind it. There have been wild speculations and statements on "Hammarskjöld's Chapel." The story is this:

I have done quite a lot of work in churches; in stained glass, mosaic, and fresco. They were mostly ancient churches, where I had to consider the problem of adding modern adornment to historical architecture. I sometimes dreamt of designing and building a small chapel of my own—decorating it my own way, without interference. My *Vence* in other words. I played with the idea of building it on my own grounds, with the help of my neighbours. We would have our own pews—we all had a long way to the nearest church. I had told Dag about this, and when we walked over the grounds of the Admiralty he stopped and said: "Why don't you build your chapel here—this would be a good place." Yes, why not?

With amazement I read what is said about "Hammarskjöld's Chapel" and its purpose, especially what has been written after *Markings* was published. Dag simply provided the site for me to do my best as an artist. His pleasure in the idea was chiefly aesthetic. We vaguely talked about its future function—probably run by a special foundation after our deaths—but we both took for granted that it would be a rather ordinary Lutheran chapel, since it was going to be built in a rather ordinary Lutheran community. At that time the Bishop of Lund was a man who wrote poetry, and Dag said: "We have to wait with the inauguration until we have a new bishop—no bad poetry!"

Dag was not a church-going person—maybe for the

Martin Buber.

reason hinted at above. We were both afraid of bad sermons, having been spoilt by growing up with great preachers like Nathan Söderblom, who was a close friend of both our families, and my father, who was constantly read in Dag's family.

If he often in *Markings* expresses himself by quoting the Bible, it is because it was natural for him to use the religious document that was part of his cultural inheritance. He once said something about having to learn to know your own country before you can have a global understanding. Likewise you have to know your inherited religion before you can begin to understand other religions. And quoting Christ does not mean that you identify yourself with him, any more than quoting Shakespeare means that you have a Hamlet-complex. He made profuse use of quotations in his addresses and speeches, and explained the reason in his Cambridge address (June 1958), after having quoted Martin Buber:

"I excuse myself for having quoted at such length. . . . I have done so because out of the depth of his feelings Martin Buber has found expressions which it would be vain for me to try to improve."

Dag never lived at Backåkra—his life was "taken from this earth" before he saw the restoration completed. In his will he left it to me to decide what pieces of art and furniture should be brought there from his home in New York or elsewhere. To keep his collection of beloved things intact, I picked far more than can be displayed at Backåkra—at present. Others have had the hard task of choosing and arranging his *objets d'art*. I have not seen the result, and I do not want to see it.

It can never give an idea of Dag's home—it must be a museum of curiosa for paying tourists to gape at.

I have sold my place and moved and started a new garden. And the chapel will probably not be built—not as we saw it.

Fires Around the Horizon

In 1958 the tempo of the political *danse macabre* began to accelerate. Dag said in his Cambridge address:

"The widening of our political horizons to embrace in a new sense the whole of the world, should have meant an approach to the ideal sung in Schiller's 'Ode to Joy'; but it has, paradoxically, led to new conflicts and to new difficulties to establish even simple human contact and communication.

"Korea, China, Indonesia, Kashmir, Palestine, Hungary, North Africa. There are fires all around the horizon, and they are not fires announcing peace."

He could have added Tunisia, Laos, Lebanon, etc., ad infinitum. Hungary really shook Dag. But as Richard I. Miller says in his excellent book *Dag Hammarskjöld and Crisis Diplomacy:*

"He could not perform miracles, as some enthusiasts were beginning to believe. Nobody could deny that he was an exceedingly able and creative diplomat, yet he could do little to achieve a political settlement in Hungary. It is not quite correct to say that Mr. Hammarskjöld failed in arranging a political settlement in Hungary; it is more accurate to say that he never had a reasonable chance for success. There is quite a difference."

In Sweden, Dag was criticised for not performing miracles, and on April 29 he wrote: "Here everything works as usual. The wheels continue to turn very rapidly, but the machine keeps going and with its vitality defies all excited claims that it never functioned and in any case now is moribund. It amuses me to see our loudest critic pronounce a death-sentence in the name of World-Federalism. It is almost like declaring dentists useless because they can't give us eternal life. But as you know, in this case the feelings are so strongly personal, that any hope of logic is out of question."

On May 3 I had a new letter: "You are quite right that the last few weeks have been rather tense. First there was the 'parade' in Jerusalem and then we got the new and very venomous conflict between the USA and the USSR. I had to play fairly high stakes in both cases with a reasonable degree of short-term success and some hopes for the future. I have sent you the texts concerning the Arctic story and I think they will tell you better than I could sum it up in a letter, how I look at the present situation. It is obvious that this seems to be one which fully warranted the risk-taking involved in the operation last Tuesday: the Russians may make big noises but there is no misunderstanding in their mind as to why I did it, and that is really all that matters for the continued work here.

"I am looking forward more and more to seeing you again in Hagestad, but I see less and less of a chance to spend there more than a weekend. But again: so what! You can squeeze a lot into a couple of days."

He did not manage to have that weekend—for "obvious reasons."

This time the reasons—the main reasons—were Lebanon and Jordan. The drawn-out, dangerous, and tricky Lebanon crisis was beginning to come under control. The third emergency special session of the General Assembly closed on August 21 after thirteen plenary sessions. Fifty-five states spoke on the issue, but as Richard I. Miller says in *Hammarskjöld and Crisis Diplomacy:* "Many statements were well reasoned and challenging, but they were presented to lightly attended Assembly meetings and had very little, if any, impact upon important meetings and negotiations that were taking place behind the scenes." And later he comments: "Mr. Hammarskjöld came out of the Lebanese crisis with more personal prestige and power than ever before."

But now Jordan was another "international tinderbox. . . . One spark might have thrown the entire Middle East into a regional war, that could have involved other powers" (Miller). Hammarskjöld flew to Jordan and surrounding states, on several trips, to prepare the ground for a settlement of the disputes, using his quiet diplomacy.

A United Nations "presence" was later established by sending a mission, headed by Pier Pasquale Spinelli. "Major credit for the eminent success of the Jordanian Mission must go to the Secretary-General. Shuttling among the various capitals during his trips in August and September of 1958, he was able to formulate a plan that was accepted by all powers concerned—a plan that represents yet another innovation in the evolution of the United Nations." (Miller)

Before leaving for Jordan on August 25, Dag wrote, on August 24: "As you well understand I have no time to write letters, but thank God I still have the possibilities to read your and other friends' letters with attention and great profit. By now I have read your latest letter many times, not only because of the interest in practical details that it stimulates, but because of the atmosphere that you convey.

"While Maria discovers the world, here we try our best to keep it in such a condition that her discoveries still are of interest when she grows up. In all the racket it is good to know that anything so real exists, as the life around Rytterskulle."

Maria was our first child, born in February 1958 "under the UN sign" as Dag wrote in an inscription on a lovely silver-cup, one of his many carefully chosen gifts to Maria. He was her godfather and took a warm interest in her doings.

In this year of many crises Dag managed to give four very important addresses, with bearing on the situation and his office. The later publication of *Markings* seems to make people forget his speeches—also published and far too little read. In 1958 he delivered them in London, Miami, Oslo, and Cambridge.

Was Hammarskjöld hard to understand, as some people say? This of course is mostly stated by those who never heard or read him—or by those with a hundred-word vocabulary. But it is quite a widespread belief. It always surprises me to hear this. I think he expressed himself very clearly—"sometimes with a dazzling clarity," to quote Toynbee in the *Observer*. Clearly for those who were in the least interested in, and had some knowledge of, what he was talking about. He had a good ear for the music of language, and he chose his words with great care, to correspond with what he wanted to say. He kept an admirable balance between the poet and the statesman —letting the one help the other.

If some people found him hard to follow—was this entirely his fault? When Dag sent me his introduction to the annual UN report (June 1958–June 1959), he wrote on the cover:

"Maybe you will be interested in these 'muddy sapiences that put you to sleep.'" (A quote from a Swedish editorial comment, by somebody who was put to a provincial sleep by the magnitude and monotony of repeated crises and difficult problems in the UN.)

Dag used to send me statements and speeches that he wanted me to read. Often they had an expressive and cryptic comment on the cover. Now and then he let me have a verbal recording of his frequent press conferences. They changed character through his time of office. When he was new in the game he delivered long, carefully prepared statements and answered all questions politely, at some length, even when they were stupid. Gradually he learned to master the technique of giving shortest possible answers to long questions, especially if they were irrelevant. The highly competent press people usually knew what to ask, and how to ask, and they respected and liked him.

But it happened that less gifted journalists took the floor. On an otherwise very interesting press conference on May 1, 1959—at the height of the Lebanese crisis!—the following question was asked:

Mr. Van Ky (*Saigon* Moi): "My second question is this. Some time ago I promised you that I would never ask you anything about your private affairs, but you remember that you told us at the last luncheon—quite aggressively you told me—'I am not married yet. Your information was wrong.'

"Now you know my English is rather poor. I did not understand everything you told me that day, but one of my colleagues wrote to me from London, and he is an Oxford man. He said: 'Mr. Hammarskjöld says that he is not married yet. That word "yet" implies that your information'—that is, my information, sir—'was not completely wrong. There must be something.' Perhaps you could give us your reaction to that?"

The Secretary-General: "At least in the personal field the Secretary-General reserves his freedom of action. But I think we can now turn to less personal questions. and I observe that you, Pete. . . ."

Poor Dag—the Van Kys of Saigon took up too much of his time and patience. They were the ones who later called him cold and distant, and hard to understand.

Between two of his rescue trips to the Middle East in the fall, he found solace in introducing Pablo Casals on UN Day, and in listening to his unsurpassed rendering of cello-suite no. 2 by Bach.

While the Jordan situation was more or less stabilized, a new minor but not negligible crisis called for attention: the growing tension between Cambodia and Thailand, with all its complicated problems, of which the ownership of the Temple of Preah Vihear was only of symbolic importance; the negotiation between the two countries broke down and Cambodia formally brought a complaint to the United Nations in the end of November. This resulted in the Beck-Friis Mission, one of the lesser-known actions of the UN, but one of great importance and with successful results. This was not much observed in the West, but it made an impact in Asia.

On November 20 Dag wrote: "I am really ashamed when I realize how long the silence on my part has been, while you on your part have, not only spent so much time and interest on the Admiralty, but also have found time to send me long, welcome letters, including excellent photos.

"As an explanation but not as an excuse I want to say that this autumn has been unlike any other. On account of this summer's adventures I was two months behind schedule when the General Assembly started its session, and this meant that I, so to speak, had to try to catch up with myself. At the same time the wheels turned quicker than ever. The result was that I was a hundred percent busy, without even a chance to get a breathing space,—something I earlier managed to find between the periods of acute crises. Whenever I had a moment free, I have under the circumstances found it natural to live entirely as a consumer and not as a producer. Pro primo this has prevented all letter-writing, and it isn't only in relation to you that I am 'behind' in a way that makes me sad.

"Enough said about this, I am convinced that you,

with your intuition for the UN and my own circumstances, have guessed this yourself. All reports from Löderup have been gleams of light and I have rejoiced in that Backåkra, our mutual child, has thrived along with Boel Maria. Have you started to think about the Chapel?

"Your own words and the photos combine to give a live impression of the activity of this summer and autumn. The solutions that you have found seem to me very satisfactory and the animated atmosphere at their execution has, to judge from the photos, been entirely in the spirit of the place. I look forward towards the time when we have succeeded in making the whole estate into what we hope for—and when I even may be allowed to live there in the future. Before somebody lives there the surroundings of course can't get their right warmth, but as far as it is humanly possible to give life to the place, you really have done everything.

"Lack of time makes it slightly difficult to comment on what is happening in this house. Everything considered I am rather satisfied. The old elephant has a surprising vitality and a very tough hide. Sometimes he stops in an alarming way but doesn't leave the road, and with suitable stimulus he starts lumbering in the right direction.

"I hope to be able to come home shortly before Christmas and then we must have occasion to fill the picture in both directions. I also ought to have a chance to see Maria, who judging from your photo, already is quite a lady."

There was no doubt about his interest in Maria and her development. On February 17, 1959, he wrote:

"It was a great joy to have your long letter yesterday,

with good news about my godchild and glimpses from the life of you and Greta.

"Today, alas, I can only send you a few short lines as a small sign of life and as thanks for both your letter and the Christmas party in your studio, which also this time had its own fine accent. I am sending you a book by Thomas Griffith as a kind of supplement to this letter. The man, who is foreign-news editor of Time, is using a few clichés and paints a bit too much in black and white, but still, he has in this book given a comment to America of today, a comment that corresponds with my own reaction after all these years. You will find it a clean and strong book with much wisdom and tenderness behind at times drastically sharp judgments."

The book was *The Waist-high Culture,* a book that represents one of the finest traditions in America: the open and intelligent criticism of what is going wrong in your own country. It also touches on art. My struggling colleagues outside the gilded racket would surely appreciate this quote:

"Have we sold our souls for a mess of pottage that goes snap, crackle and pop?"

Laos

The year 1959 did not start well. The new year certainly did not mean any diminishing of the fires around the horizon.

In his address at the Atoms for Peace Award ceremony on January 29 Hammarskjöld said: "The voice of the political leaders now can penetrate to the innermost recesses of what was *terra incognita* only some decades ago. Members of a family who starves in the Indo-Chinese jungle nowadays are people we all may meet. It is no longer a feat to visit the clay-huts of the desert. And we have no excuse not to tackle with our modern equipment the diseases of children in the igloos of the arctic region."

His actions corresponded with his words. On March 2 he landed in Pakistan, the first stop on a long inspection tour, that took him to Burma, Thailand, Laos, Cambodia, Malaya, Nepal, Afghanistan, and ended in the Soviet, with the famous rowing-trip with Khrushchev on the Black Sea.

At a press-conference on his return he was asked what happened on the row-boat trip and which language they used. Hammarskjöld answered: "It was a very pleasant trip. We were certainly united in our love of the sea. The language was the language of the sea. That is to say, you can point out directions, and for the rest, faces can express the pleasure one takes in the trip." This answer was fully worthy of a diplomat, and in the true spirit of the Zen-masters Kwam and Kwat.

Later he told us that Khrushchev had taken the oars and Dag had pointed out the direction. Khrushchev had said: "When I come to visit you we will row again, but then you will have to row, and I will tell you where to go." Dag's answer was: "Well, in that case we will each take one oar!"

In a letter of April 11 he wrote about the trip:

"The voyage went well and gave fantastic experiences, partly encouraging, partly very frightening. The climax: a private evening with Khrushchev (with a *very* animated discussion of Pasternak), a flight in a small aircraft around the giants of Eastern Himalaya and a day in Arcadia by the upper Mekong in the ancient kingdom of Luang Prabang. I have much to tell you on Rytters-kulle.

"*A great* experience: how much more mature and fine the Asiastic art of living is compared to ours. Evidently you have to accept the thought that everything is an illusion, before you can master the whole scale of reality with ease, style, seriousness and happiness. What does it then matter if you are poor, politically ignorant or threatened."

On April 28 another letter—this time a short one:

"Hope to see you on the 5th or 6th—as a better and fuller greeting I am sending you what I intend to say in Copenhagen and Lund—in the Lund address I am trying to unburden myself of an old debt, you will see that it is strongly felt and very seriously meant—."

In Lund he said (*inter alia*):

"To a Westerner of a later generation who is facing Asia and Africa of today, it is a useful exercise to go back to the works about these areas written by distinguished Europeans, whose mental attitude was shaped in the main before the first World War. What strikes one in the first place is, perhaps, how much they did *not* see and did *not* hear, and how even their most positive attempts at entering into a world of different thoughts and emotions were coloured by an unthinking, self-assured superiority.

"To an increasing extent, experts from the West have gone out to the new nations in Asia and Africa to help the governments in different posts. In this, they have embarked on a career entirely in the spirit of the age, and one which belongs to the future—not as some kind of missionaries either for the West or for a world community, but in order to serve, by practical work, the evolution towards the synthesis which is on the way. . . . They should realize that it is a sign of the highest culture to be really capable of listening, learning and therefore also responding in a way which helps less favoured ones; while it is a privilege reserved for the half-educated, who is unaware of his limitations, to be a poor listener in a feeling of his own false superiority—."

After having delivered the Lund address he came to

Greta,

　　med stor sakamat och inte de Dis,
tillsammans med alla vänner och
varma hälsningar till Maria och
Dig själv.

Dag.

5 maj. 59.

From his many photos of Himalaya, Dag gave me this one. To Greta, who for some reason could not join us for luncheon, he sent a Buddha from Bangkok with this inscription: "Greta, with deep regret not to see you with all my friends and with warm greetings to Maria and yourself."

Dag entertains his godchild, Maria, by drawing a picture of what the summers looked like in his childhood.

Stockholm for a day, and gave a luncheon for a few friends. As usual, he did not touch on the seriousness of his Middle East voyage in March—or on its results— but told us enthusiastically of other experiences. Both from "high-altitude" and "from going from village to village." He showed us photos, his own excellent photos, from his flight among the giants of Eastern Himalaya, and added smiling that he had asked the pilot over and over again to take another turn for more shots, until they suddenly realized that the small aircraft had lost height. At the last moment they managed to climb out over a pass.

His description of Laos was pure poetry—he told us of life on upper Mekong, where everybody lived on boats and instead of verbal communication played messages on flutes; a language of music like birds singing in paradise. He later gave me a reed-flute—it still has a strange fragrance of the East—and a lovely tone.

This "paradise" was in serious trouble. The later Vietnam crisis was already throwing a shadow. The whole Middle East was in a turmoil, but Laos was at the moment the obvious spot of eruption. The tension grew during the spring and summer and reached a dangerous peak in the autumn, seemed under control in the spring of 1960, but exploded again and was one of the many "unsolved" problems that Dag never was allowed to forget.

Between his many voyages in the summer of 1959 he managed to give himself two weekends in Hagestad, when passing by. "You can squeeze a lot into a couple of days!" He inspected the Admiralty and his godchild Maria—found both developing in a satisfactory way—

he drew plans for the Admiralty and pictures for Maria. She still has one, where he showed her what his childhood's summers looked like: a boy fishing, a horse-carriage on the way to a rickety wooden landing-stage below a red-painted cottage with a flag, a cow, a rowboat, small white clouds, and a big sun. An enormous swan and an old lady complete the picture.

Dag took care of every minute—and he certainly needed these few days of normal life. He turned back to difficult sessions on the Laos crisis, and when the tension in that particular area seemed diminished—for the time being—he started on his long African tour on December 21. As usual several moves ahead of what later was to develop into the Congo-crisis.

[153]

Maria's thick blunt crayons gave Dag difficulties with details, but the flag is no doubt the blue UN flag —a rather nice anachronism— probably to remind Maria that she was born "under this sign".

Dag Hammerskjöld 1959:

"My childhood summer". Crayon on paper, 8⅝ by 10⅝ inches, private collection.

Tanganyika, January 1960.

Africa

"The Congolese surge toward independence may have caught Belgium unaware but not Hammarskjöld. Almost from the first day he assumed office he had been alive to the new stirrings in Africa and their importance to the UN." (Lash: *Dag Hammarskjöld.*)

His extensive African tour from December 1959–January 1960 took Hammarskjöld (in slightly more than a month) to Senegal, Liberia, Guinea, Ghana, Togoland, Nigeria, British Cameroons, Congo (Brazaville, Leopoldville, Stanleyville), Ruanda-Urundi, Tanganyika, Kenya, Uganda, Somaliland, Ethiopia, Eritrea, Sudan, Egypt, Libya, Tunisia—in this order—and ended in Morocco. There he was received with a specially composed march in his honour, and he spoke at the United Nations Economic Commission for Africa:

". . . The image I take back with me is a refreshing one of youth and vigour, and generally speaking, of a remarkable aptitude on the part of the leaders to grasp facts and adhere to facts, not-withstanding the understandable impatience and the strong ideological currents which are necessary ingredients of the rapid changes now taking place. . . ."

He had met and listened to the leaders of the young nations, and he told me how he had found intelligent young men who gave him hope for the future. A future full of difficulties and dangers.

In an address at the University of Chicago Law School he gave a warning of what he saw ahead (May 1, 1960):

"On this point a word of warning may be in order. The fact that important sections of the Charter—I think especially of Chapter VII which lays down the rules for intervention of the UN with military forces—so far have not been implemented—does not mean that on these points we are facing a dead letter."

Two months later, on June 30, the Belgian Congo had its day of independence. In July there was already complete chaos, and Lumumba appealed to the UN for military assistance to the Congolese Government, while Belgium was sending 3500 more soldiers to reinforce their troops in an "independent" Congo. The Secretary-General called an emergency meeting of the Security Council on July 13—and the result of a two days' dramatic session was the setting up of a second United Nations Emergency Force.

This was only the military side of an effectively organized rescue-action to rush help and assistance to Congo. Busy with solving practical problems, Hammarskjöld was under heavy fire politically. His line of

Nigeria, December 1959.

neutrality and scrupulous adherence to the aims and principles of the UN, as usual made him enemies among the Big Powers, in East and West. Everybody told Hammarskjöld what to do. "Something must be done!" Yes—evidently.

Hammarskjöld, while listening to all demands shouted at him in the UN debates, maybe heard himself repeat his oath of office:

I, Dag Hammarskjöld, solemnly swear—not to seek or accept instruction in regard to the performance of my duties from any government or other authority external to the Organization.

Patiently and clearly, in statement after statement, in session after session, he explained the situation, and the possibilities—or lack of possibilities—of the UN and the Secretary-General to act "in strict accordance with the principles and purposes of the Charter." But he was always trying to find a way—a way of acting a bit in advance of resolutions. "I have no other choice than to follow my own conviction."

"To the best of my understanding I have acted as swiftly as is humanly possible." Sometimes he did more than was humanly possible, as all those who worked with him at that time have witnessed. The lights were on all night on the 38th floor, and the "Congo-Club" has many stories to tell about his unbelievable endurance, patience, and sense of humour, in moments of tiredness and despair in his collaborators.

Dag dealt with all big crises and serious attacks on him and his office with polite firmness, invulnerable in his strict adherence to the principles of the Charter. On

Katanga, August 14, 1960.

this level he could meet almost everything with fortitude. But the hits below the belt of a more personal kind, delivered by provincial and small minds (in Sweden and elsewhere), could hurt him deeply. This will surprise those who called him "hard." He was an extremely sensitive and vulnerable person, forced by his office and duty to hard decisions and firm action. Of him could be said what Carl Sandburg said on the 150th anniversary of Lincoln's birth:

> Not often in the story of mankind does a man arrive on earth who is both steel and velvet . . .

In a statement before Security Council on August 21, 1960, Dag said in a debate on the Congo:

"In order to carry out my mandate, I have been forced to act with great firmness in relation to many parties. One of them has been the central government itself. I do not believe that I ever failed in courtesy. On the other hand, I do not excuse myself for having stated clearly the principles of the Charter and for having acted independently on their basis, mindful of the dignity of the organization—and to have done so whether it suited all those we are trying to help or not." After continuing with a long and detailed report of the situation, he ended with a characteristic proof of his sense of proportions: "In the perspective just outlined, the tension of the moment disappears and even the Belgian intervention and the Security Council counter-action are reduced to an episode. This meeting of the Security Council would rise above the reasons which have made it necessary if we were to look towards the real problems of the future. The need of the moment may falsify our perspectives. It seems to me to be the time to look ahead and to brush aside those conflicts and divergencies of views and emotions, which for so long have delayed a concentrated effort to mold the people of the Congo into a happy and prosperous state, adding to the stability and progress of Africa and thereby contributing to the peace of the world."

But he spoke to deaf ears. The attacks on Hammarskjöld culminated at the by now famous General Assembly meeting of September 20, 1960, when many heads of state personally came to New York to swing the hatchet. A very grave and tense Dag answered the Russian demand that he should resign, in a controlled and impassioned voice, with a well-known and often quoted speech. When he came to the words: "I shall remain in my post"—he was interrupted by a deafening applause with some effort cut short by Dag who repeated:

"I shall remain in my post during the term of my office as a servant of the organization in the interest of all those other nations, as long as *they* wish me to do so.

"In this context the representative of the Soviet Union spoke of courage. It is very easy to resign; it is not so easy to stay on. It is very easy to bow to the wish of a big Power. It is another matter to resist. As is well known to all members of this Assembly, I have done so before on many occasions and in many directions. If it is the wish of those nations who see in the organization their best protection in the present world, I shall now do so again."

When he had finished his speech with these words, the delegates rose to their feet and gave him an ovation, that

In the General Assembly, September 29, 1960.

Castro and Khrushchev—General Assembly
September 20, 1960.

was the longest in the history of the UN. This manifestation was greatly improved by the Russian delegation, pounding at their desk with both fists, happily smiling. (Not using their shoes on this occasion, as a popular story goes. They may have used this nice old custom from the time of the Czars on other occasions.)

Dag remained in his post, and the situations he had to tackle got worse and multiplied unendingly. Congo was the darkest and longest chapter in the history of the UN up to then—it will be written and rewritten over and over again, as new material comes to light. I have to refrain even from trying, and limit myself to Dag and his situation, in his own words; he summed it up in a letter on December 20, 1960:

"I live in a kind of Congo-inferno, where I have not a moment for myself."

At the start of the fatal year of 1961 I had a cable:

IN THIS RUGGED BEGINNING OF THE NEW YEAR
GREETINGS LIKE YOURS ARE DOUBLY WELCOME WARM-
EST GOOD WISHES

DAG

And on January 27 he wrote:

"Warm thanks for your letter of the 21st that reached me at the end of a very trying day—one in a long succession—with threatening changes in the situation and difficult decisions. As usual—or perhaps more than usual —it did me a lot of good and I felt it as a strong personal encouragement. Thank God that you let your pen flow in this manner; it gives me a personal contact that almost is equal to being together.

"*Who does he think he is—a man of destiny?*"

"I will not comment on what is happening here, above what I have already said. My comments of today would be very bitter, and this goes both for East and West, and both for Africa and Asia. We are far from a world where even a true national interest leads to the individual subordinating himself, not to mention how far we are from the stage, where a question of vital international interest is given the superiority over a national one.

"I can tell you that your image-fantasies around *Chronique* really were appreciated by Saint-John Perse. . . ."

"Chronique"
and "The Antiphon"

Dag seemed to have had a few moments for himself before the Congo-inferno developed its full force. As usual he used them to rest temporarily tired parts of his brain, and fortify himself by literary activity. He had found time to work on a translation of *Chronique* by Saint-John Perse.

In the summer of 1960 he sent me the first completed translation, dated August 8, the date of a stormy Security Council meeting where the resolution to order Belgian troops out of Katanga was adopted.

This translation of *Chronique* was made for the Swedish Academy, by the member "Herr Hammarskjöld," with a suggestion that Saint-John Perse should have the Nobel Prize in literature. It was later published with many changes, suggested by his literary friends. I liked his first draft better. There are two ways of translating. Either you keep yourself in the background and try your best to make the poet speak in a new and

Alexis Léger.

strange language. Or you write your own highly personal poetry, where the original author only furnishes the material. Dag was the first kind of translator—but being something of a poet himself, he gave his faithful rendering the right tone. He was too humble, in my opinion, in letting others tamper with his first inspired translation. Maybe it had its faults—but they were nice faults.

I was fascinated by *Chronique*. Its strange cosmic timelessness, touching on all civilizations and situations of man—a story of man and earth and creation—started me off on a serial of monotypes, which is still being added to from time to time. Every stanza in that extraordinary lovely poem is a challenge to me as a painter.

Alexis Léger (Saint-John Perse) received the Nobel Prize in literature for 1960. He came to Stockholm and I had a cable from Dag: "Help save Vieux Maître from overmuch officialdom."

We tried. Alexis Léger and his sweet wife Dorothy came for luncheon. Alexis is an intensively alive and aware person, with an eye and ear for everything around him. We had moved into two small 150-year-old houses with a garden, overlooking the harbour and waterway entrance to Stockholm. Alexis and Maria, two years old, struck an immediate friendship; they pressed their noses flat against the windowpanes and watched the boats.

Dag had told him about my fantasies around *Chronique*, and he asked for them. I spread them out over the floor, and he and Maria crawled on all fours and made comments. Alexis finally turned to his wife and said, "This is what I want!" He told me that the publishing firm of Gallimard had asked him for a *de luxe* collection of *Chronique*, illustrated. They had proposed several of the more known contemporary artists, but Alexis Léger had so far refused.

In the letter of December 20 about the Congo-inferno, Dag also said: "Yesterday I had a letter about the luncheon with Perse and his wife. How I envy you,— and how happy I am over what the letters tell! I am eager to see what you have made out of *Chronique*. Also curious to have Perse's own reactions. His rapidly changing images with their core of reality must be very hard to catch. But for you as for me the deciding fact is the inner communication."

Alexis Léger and Dag had much in common. For being a "cold and friendless" man Dag had an amazing lot of friends. It is often said of him: "Even his friends could not get near him." Well—what friends? And how near did they try to push themselves? He was certainly not the back-slapping, embracing kind, but even when he kept a physical distance, his mental closeness could be very great. He had friends in many fields and on many levels, among those a normal amount of "close friends"—a few at the UN, a few outside, some in the field of science and art, some just nice ordinary people. "For you as for me the deciding fact is the inner communication."

Chronique had been published in Sweden with Dag's translation. The critics faithfully did their duty as the slaves of Caesar and reminded him of his limitations. Dag wrote (December 23): "God knows if it was wise to agree to its publication! On the whole I am satisfied with the translation but it could have been allowed to mature some more. However: there it is and maybe somebody finds it helpful.

Djuna Barnes.

"What I have seen of the reviews is what I expected —with some surprise, however, over the complaints that I have been insensitive to the melody of language or 'not engaged' [sic]. I am interested to see how they judge *Antiphon* now in January. In a few days I am off to Africa again. —It is a bit hard after this autumn of death-dance and without any rest, but necessity knows no law and developments are not waiting for my convenience."

"Not engaged!" This is one of the phrases the young critics of today like to throw out, when their own lack of maturity makes them miss the finer points of a mature work. The kind where all traces of hard labour are erased, where the result is clear and controlled and seems so easily arrived at. I have said before—and I repeat, that Dag's deep engagement in whatever he was doing never took the form of big gestures and loud noises. He was called self-centered and unengaged by people of limited minds and senses.

The Antiphon is the play by Djuna Barnes, an *œuvre poétique* that Dag had translated into Swedish in collaboration with Karl Ragnar Gierow, then head of the Royal Dramatic Theatre in Stockholm, where it was later produced. An interesting production of a fascinating drama.

Gierow tells about meeting Djuna Barnes in Dag's home in New York: ". . . a lady dressed in black who, with her impressive face and her walking-stick, seemed rather like Miranda in *The Antiphon*." The Scotch poet and critic Edwin Muir had called the then unpublished drama one of the most important of our time—and when Dag happened to walk beside Muir in the pro-

Jadis des hommes de haut site . . . nous ont dansé sans
gestes danse immobile de l'aigle. (*Alexis Léger himself
struck this pose to show me the dance of the eagle.*)

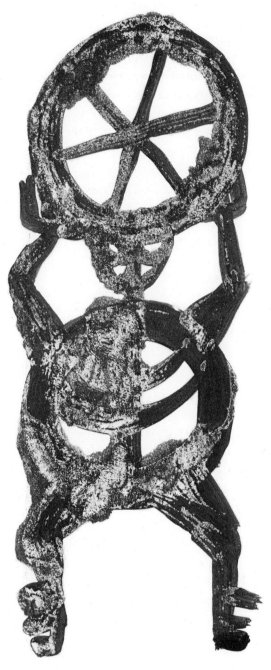

(*From* "*Chronique*") "Et la roue tourne entre nos mains,
comme au tambour de pierre de l'Aztèque."

cession on receiving one of Dag's many academic honorary degrees, they talked about *The Antiphon* all the way.

As usual Dag had chosen to tackle an exclusive and far from easy masterpiece. As a Stockholm critic wrote: "This exquisite and strange poem, that Djuna Barnes has written without a thought of how limited the power of reception is in the public. . . . The magic she exerts is felt in the resplendent translation."

The inmates of the Doll's House in *The Antiphon* could not be stranger than the figures Dag had to watch and deal with in the mad puppet show around him.

> . . . I'll sit this out.
> Do I hear the world approaching at my back?
> Then though the world be present, I'll be proctor—
> Hurry! Hurry! This way for the toymen:
> This way, strutters . . .
>
> (Jack Blow in *The Antiphon*)

The *danse macabre* in Congo went on and on, with complicated choreography and rapidly changing prima donnas. Dag's letters from this period always start with apologies for not writing more often:

April 9, 1961—"You will understand that when I get off the hook, I kind of sink back into passivity, which in due time, I hope, will be reasonably fertile, but which for the moment represents a somewhat barren land as human contacts and correspondence go.

"You will have received a copy of my reply to the Russians. It covers the ground psychologically and I don't need to give you any further comments on the situation here, as far as my affairs are concerned. I think the operation has succeeded for the third time. And that is alright, but it is boring to have to deal with these continued attacks in which I have to operate for purely defensive purposes, a thing I dislike quite heartily. . . ."

Of April 22 I had another letter, ending with some good news: "Six o'clock this morning we buried the 15th session of the General Assembly after various political and moral strip-tease acts—performed by less than well-shaped personalities. Now I guess I should 'relax' for some 24 hours before trying to tidy up everything that has been deranged during this strange session which, anyway from my point of view, was fruitful since the wear and tear process, which the Russians tried on me and my position, did not work while it proved highly effective with regard to their own impact on the Afro-Asians. This showed up just as well yesterday night as Saturday a week ago when they tried a vote of confidence which flopped hopelessly. . . .

"I was happy to hear that Wally has approached you! For the time being the Library is just a skeleton and it will take some time before you can get an idea about the room. . . ."

Wallace Harrison had suggested that I should be asked to paint a mural in the pent-house room of the new UN Library, a four-story building attached as a wing to the Secretariat sky-scraper. This glass-walled room was like an aquarium at the bottom of a valley in the crazy rock-landscape of towering sky-scrapers. I chose to build my "composition for concave wall" on microscopic things, such as planktons and crystal-forms. In times of silly moon-rockets and science-fiction the luxe for overgrown children, I thought it was time to call attention to the infinitely more fascinating microcosm that is the nucleus of our world, its creation and its future.

I got plans and measurements of the pent-house room, made a model of it, and started sketching. From then on I was submerged in my microcosm and only made a break to go to New York and show some sketches.

The Last Summer

Around Midsummer 1961 I stayed with Dag for a week. I found 'him changed. More tired, restless, and pessimistic than I had ever seen him. He evidently was glad to see me—and the sketches for the Library-mural. But the last year had left a mark on him.

I asked as I used to do on meeting him again, "Do you still have faith in man?" Meaning the individual on his own, not in mobs or masses or political parties. Dag had always up to then answered positively, but this time he looked sad and pensive and he said, "No, I never thought it possible, but lately I have come to understand that there are really evil persons—evil right through—only evil."

I also found a changed UN. The situation up on the 38th floor was changed. Being under attack for having too many Western Under-Secretaries, Dag had been forced to do some re-organization. To make it easier for him, Andrew Cordier had resigned. Andy—who had been the pillar of strength and the foundation of the house for such a long time! Dag had already appointed his successor as Chef du Cabinet: the Indian diplomat C. V. Narasimhan. Dag gave a luncheon on the 38th floor, with Ralph Bunche, Andy Cordier, Narasimhan, Wieschhoff (who later crashed with him in Ndola), and two very nice young African diplomats, who sat on either side of Dag. Dag was tense and nervous, and covered it up by a constant flow of brilliant conversation with his African guests. In French, which few of us could follow. In the relative silence at the other end of the table I could feel undercurrents that made that luncheon a sad affair, in spite of all gallant efforts to keep smiling.

Dag was more tied up than ever, and more desperate over wasted time with "important" visitors, who, as Dag said, took up his time only to be able to go home and say, "I had a most interesting talk with the Secretary-General, most important." He had at least one visitor though who gave him great pleasure: Alexis Léger. I found the two friends, for a moment relaxing in the private-talk corner of Dag's office, talking of things worth talking about.

He managed to get up to Brewster over the weekend. This time he brought two security officers, Bill and Victor, and his new butler, Edin, whom he had met as the chief-steward of his plane on the African tour. As usual we went out to the raft, and Dag carried books to read. But Bill had built a speed-boat and now he also brought water-skis. The boys had quite a rumpus, while Dag tried to concentrate on his reading.

Andy Cordier—last day in office.

Before we drove up, Dag had confessed that he was tired. "If I have *one* unsolvable problem to think of night and day, I can manage, and even so if I have two or three at the same time—but when they keep multiplying, my brain starts to boil. I simply have to find something good and hard to translate. But what?" We discussed Julien Gracq, Martin Buber, and a few others. With him to Brewster, Dag had brought both Martin Buber and Julien Gracq.

He tried to settle down to his much-longed-for reading in the stillness of the lake. No stillness that day! I kept him company on the raft, but the other three kept going full speed in the motor-boat, round and round the raft, that rocked and rolled and was sprayed with cascades of water. Finally the vigorous crew began to land on the raft and start from there. Bill was trying to teach Edin the noble art of water-skiing. More yelling and splashing. Dag's whole body expressed intense concentration and disgust. At last Bill sensed that something was wrong, and he kindly asked Dag, "Would you like to try this, sir?" "No, thank you, I am reading," was Dag's answer, and he added, "At least I am *trying* to!"

We all took the hint, silently boarded the boat, and with muffled motor sneaked back to the landing stage. Bill's comment was: "Coming here to swim and have fun—and then: reading books!"

We sat in the green half-light of the overhanging trees and watched the shadows grow longer and longer, until they finally reached the solitary figure out on the raft, and it was time to have supper. As usual we ate in candlelight and afterwards had coffee and a good old brandy under the stars and fireflies outside. The others being busy in the kitchen, Dag and I had our last long talk. He kept commenting on his physical fitness, as if he wanted to reassure himself—but we also talked about death—a thought that none of us was afraid of. He had made his last will many years ago, and we agreed that you owe it to others to leave everything in as good order as possible. I asked him if he had kept some kind of diary. Dag said, "A political diary—no—but I have from time to time written some other things." I cannot recall his exact words, and I am reluctant to try to reconstruct other talks we had on subjects touching on religion and philosophy. I cannot trust my memory, and maybe the reason is that we generally agreed—if we had had different basic opinions or had quarrelled I may have remembered it.

I do remember that we talked some more about evil. Not the triumphant evil of the Devil and the generals, with their blazing sins, big and clear as an atom blast. There is another kind of evil that creeps and seeps and nags and undermines, trying to get you like quicksand. It has a sweet rotten smell of decay and defeat and false love, it calls for pity and sympathy—and cries for help, when it fails in pulling others down in the bog. There is no help for this kind of evil—no cure.

I asked Dag if he ever had had any experience of this deceptive brand of evil, and he answered: "Yes, I know too well what you are talking about. I have had this problem—quite near." We fell silent for a while, and I did not ask him more.

The crickets made us conscious of the silence, and the darkness was intensified by the fireflies. The words that fell between us were probably not important

[185]

in themselves—they were signs of good will to communicate, punctuating the intervals of silent thought. Silence in company with Dag was never a void. It was always filled; this time with more sadness and pessimism than I ever had felt—or understood—before this last night at Brewster. Being torn apart by the demands on him as Secretary-General, he had a need to return to his core of privacy. I felt this very strongly, but at the same time I felt he was retiring into an abstract world.

We sat late into the hot summer night and we talked some more—we were both in a mood of confessions and reminiscences. Next morning Dag was up early; he had acquired a habit of almost not sleeping at all. Don Thomas later told me that on the last weekends at Brewster he sat up all night, listening to the birds and watching the sunrise. And from Sture Linnér I heard that Dag's bed was not touched on the last night before the flight to Ndola.

That Sunday morning in Brewster, Dag was in a very black mood, maybe because we had to return to New York, maybe because he had had bad news on the hot line to head-quarters. No sense to ask him: What is the matter? Best to leave him alone. It was one of those days when nothing helped—even Bill couldn't do anything about it. We all felt it was our fault—and drove home in silence. I was to leave for Sweden the next day and I thought: I am too tired to do anything about it now—I will try to make up for it on my return, when we have plenty of time. (I expected to stay with Dag several months while doing my mural in the Library.)

How was I to know that I would never see him again? (The next time I saw Brewster, an enormous and fully equipped space-ship was floating in the dining room. I passed Brewster in the spring of 1966 on my way north with Brian Urquhart. He had never seen Dag's place and we paid a brief visit. The Indian lake was deserted and black. But the house was full of life and noise—an extremely nice family with lots of children had moved into it. They knew vaguely about the former tenant, but did not care much. I found the new spirit of the place rather nice—I was glad to see it filled with life and not turned into a memorial.)

For the rest of this summer, 1961, Dag's letters were full of concern with practical matters which he wanted me to attend to. "God knows I am not too fussy about such practical matters, but as nobody knows when anything happens . . ." There has been much talk about Dag's "premonitions" and why he made careful arrangements, "as if he expected to die." Of course he expected to die. He was no exception from the fact that we have every day on loan, and in his position he must have been more conscious of this than most mortals. Besides—he was a very orderly person. He wrote:

"It was most kind of you to go to such length both in replying to me and in making all kinds of safety arrangements. What was back of my reaction was only the feeling of responsibility I always have in an existence of the uttermost uncertainty; it is a kind of protection to know that all things which may be of practical importance are well in hand independently of what may happen to me."

[187]

The End

What happened at Ndola? Maybe the truth will be known one day, since there are "human factors" involved, who may tell what they know sooner or later —boasting over a drink or confessing on a death-bed. Maybe the charcoal-burners who saw a second, attacking aircraft were telling the truth—what reasons had they to lie? Why was the wreckage not officially found until fifteen hours after the crash?

> Secretary-General Dag Hammarskjöld's body was the only one of those found dead on the scene of the accident which had completely escaped burning. . . . The result of the post-mortem indicates that he lived for a certain time after the crash.
>
> (Report from Swedish medical experts.)

As regards search and rescue action, the commission notes that, although SE-BDY crashed 9.5 miles from an airfield on which eighteen military aircraft capable of

From the site of the crash.

carrying out an air search were stationed, the wreckage was located by the Rhodesian authorities only 15 hours after the crash and more than 9 hours after first light September 18, 1961.

(From the UN commission's report.)

Whatever happened is irreparable. A good man died with his comrades, and I would like to quote his own words on the death of a Swedish poet and friend, in a letter of August 6, 1961:

He was indeed one of the few and perhaps last representatives of a spiritual standard, a natural nobility, a warmth of heart and an iron-clad integrity, which is more necessary than ever in the present period of growing darkness and decay. How many of his poems do not take on a new significance in the light of his last difficult years and his end.

PHOTO CREDITS

ABOUT THIS BOOK

The text is set in Linotype Janson, which dates from about 1700 and is probably of Dutch origin. Palatino, designed by Herman Lapf seemed most appropriate for the display type. Design format and layout of illustrations was done by Earl Tidwell in collaboration with Joseph P. Ascherl and the editorial assistance of Elizabeth Drew.